EYEWITNESS

WORLD

WAR I

WITHDRAWN

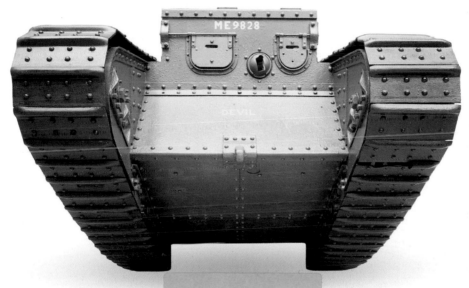

Signboard from Ypres station, 1916

Early British reconnaissance aircraft

Book that stopped a bullet

Early gas helmet

British "carcass" incendiary bomb

British 9 kg (20 lb) Hales bomb

French tin soldiers

German incendiary bomb, dropped during first air raid on London

Model of British motor ambulance used on the Western Front

Prussian
Iron Cross

EYEWITNESS
WORLD
WAR I

Written by
SIMON ADAMS

Photographed by
ANDY CRAWFORD

US Distinguished
Service Cross

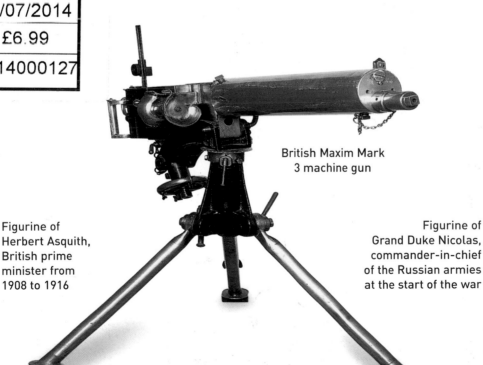

British Maxim Mark
3 machine gun

Figurine of
Herbert Asquith,
British prime
minister from
1908 to 1916

Figurine of
Grand Duke Nicolas,
commander-in-chief
of the Russian armies
at the start of the war

IN ASSOCIATION WITH
THE IMPERIAL WAR MUSEUM

British officer's compass

German steel helmet adapted for use with a telephone

Dummy rifles used by British army recruits, 1914–15

LONDON, NEW YORK,
MELBOURNE, MUNICH, AND DELHI

Project editor Patricia Moss
Art editors Julia Harris, Rebecca Painter
Senior editor Monica Byles
Senior art editors Jane Tetzlaff, Clare Shedden
Category publisher Jayne Parsons
Managing art editor Jacquie Gulliver
Senior production controller Kate Oliver
Picture research Sean Hunter
DTP designers Justine Eaton, Matthew Ibbotson

RELAUNCH EDITION (DK UK)
Editor Ashwin Khurana
Senior designers Rachael Grady, Spencer Holbrook
Managing editor Gareth Jones
Managing art editor Philip Letsu
Publisher Andrew Macintyre
Producer (pre-production) Adam Stoneham
Senior producer Charlotte Cade
Jacket editor Manisha Majithia
Jacket designer Laura Brim
Jacket design development manager Sophia MTT
Publishing director Jonathan Metcalf
Associate publishing director Liz Wheeler
Art director Phil Ormerod

RELAUNCH EDITION (DK INDIA)
Senior editor Neha Gupta
Art editor Deep Shikha Walia
Senior DTP designer Harish Aggarwal
DTP designers Anita Yadav, Pawan Kumar
Managing editor Alka Thakur Hazarika
Managing art editor Romi Chakraborty
CTS manager Balwant Singh
Jacket editorial manager Saloni Talwar
Jacket designers Govind Mittal, Suhita Dharamjit, Vikas Chauhan

This Eyewitness ® Guide has been conceived by
Dorling Kindersley Limited and Editions Gallimard
First published in Great Britain in 2001
This relaunch edition published in 2014 by
Dorling Kindersley Limited, 80 Strand, London WC2R 0RL

Copyright © 2001, © 2004, © 2007, © 2014
Dorling Kindersley Limited
A Penguin Random House Company

2 4 6 8 10 9 7 5 3 1
196564 – July/14

A CIP catalogue record for this book is
available from the British Library.

ISBN 978-1-4093-4366-0

Colour reproduction by Alta Image Ltd., London, UK
Printed by South China Printing Co. Ltd., China

Discover more at
www.dk.com

French *Croix de Guerre* medal awarded for valour

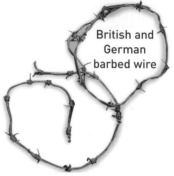

British and German barbed wire

British steel helmet with visor

Grenade

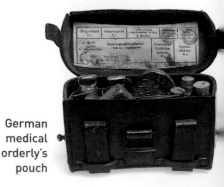

German medical orderly's pouch

Contents

High-explosive shells

Divided Europe

At the start of the 20th century, the countries of Europe were increasingly hostile to one another. While Britain, France, and Germany vied for trade and influence, Austria-Hungary and Russia both tried to dominate the Balkan states of southeast Europe. Military alliances, a naval arms race, and two Balkan wars in 1912–13 made the political situation tense, but few predicted a war.

HMS *Dreadnought*

Britain's HMS *Dreadnought*, launched in 1906, outperformed every other battleship of the day. As a result, Germany, France, and other maritime nations, began to build their own "Dreadnoughts", starting a worldwide naval armaments race.

Kaiser Wilhelm II

On becoming kaiser (emperor) of Germany in 1888, Wilhelm II tried to turn Germany into a world power, but his aggressive policies and arrogant behaviour upset other European nations, particularly Britain and France.

HMS Dreadnought *had a top speed of 21 knots*

Hand-painted, tinplate toy battleship

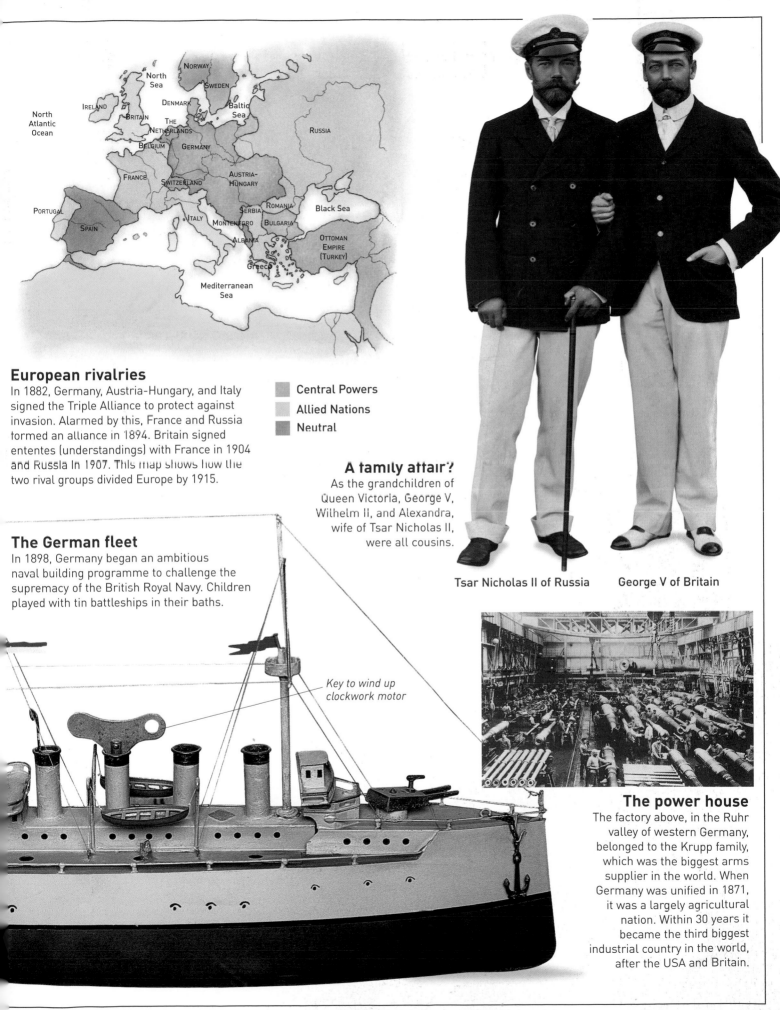

European rivalries

In 1882, Germany, Austria-Hungary, and Italy signed the Triple Alliance to protect against invasion. Alarmed by this, France and Russia formed an alliance in 1894. Britain signed ententes (understandings) with France in 1904 and Russia in 1907. This map shows how the two rival groups divided Europe by 1915.

Central Powers
Allied Nations
Neutral

A family affair?

As the grandchildren of Queen Victoria, George V, Wilhelm II, and Alexandra, wife of Tsar Nicholas II, were all cousins.

Tsar Nicholas II of Russia   George V of Britain

The German fleet

In 1898, Germany began an ambitious naval building programme to challenge the supremacy of the British Royal Navy. Children played with tin battleships in their baths.

Key to wind up clockwork motor

The power house

The factory above, in the Ruhr valley of western Germany, belonged to the Krupp family, which was the biggest arms supplier in the world. When Germany was unified in 1871, it was a largely agricultural nation. Within 30 years it became the third biggest industrial country in the world, after the USA and Britain.

A fatal shot

The assassins
Gavrilo Princip, above right, fired the fatal shot that sparked the Great War.

On 28 June 1914, the heir to the Austro-Hungarian throne, Archduke Franz Ferdinand, was shot dead in Sarajevo, Bosnia. As Bosnia was claimed by neighbouring Serbia, Austria-Hungary blamed Serbia for the assassination, and on 28 July declared war. Germany supported Austria-Hungary, Russia supported Serbia, and France supported Russia. When Germany invaded neutral Belgium on its way to France, Britain declared war on Germany. The Great War had begun.

The Austro-Hungarian army
The Austro-Hungarian empire had three armies – Austrian, Hungarian, and the "Common Army". Ten main languages were spoken, leading to frequent communication difficulties.

Bomb bounced off canopy and landed under following car

Archduke and his wife Sophie sat in the back of the open-top car

Princip fired at close range from the running board

Austro-Hungarian *Reiter* (Trooper) of the 8th Uhlan (Lancer) Regiment

Mobilize!
In July 1914, military notices across Europe told citizens that their country was being mobilized (prepared) for war, and that all regular and reserve troops should report for duty.

Germany rejoices
Germany mobilized on 1 August, declaring war against Russia that evening and against France on 3 August. Many civilians rushed to join the army in support of Kaiser and country.

One day in Sarajevo
Believing that Bosnia should be part of Serbia, six assassins ambushed Archduke Ferdinand on route to the Austrian governor's residence in Sarajevo. One threw a bomb at Ferdinand's car, but it bounced off and exploded minutes later. When Ferdinand and his wife went to visit the injured officers in hospital, Gavrilo Princip mounted the royal car and shot the couple.

28 June Archduke Franz Ferdinand is assassinated
5 July Germany gives its ally, Austria-Hungary, total support

23 July Austria issues an ultimatum to Serbia that threatens Serbian independence

25 July Serbia agrees to most of the demands
28 July Austria-Hungary ignores Serbia's terms and declares war

30 July Russia mobilizes in support of its ally, Serbia
1 August Germany mobilizes against Russia and declares

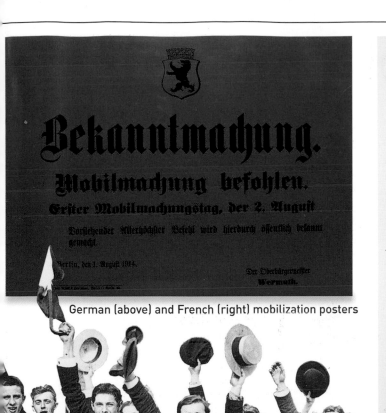

Bekanntmachung.
Mobilmachung befohlen.
Erster Mobilmachungstag, der 2. August

Vorstehender Allerhöchster Befehl wird hierdurch öffentlich bekannt gemacht.

Berlin, den 1. August 1914.

Der Oberbürgermeister
Wermuth.

German (above) and French (right) mobilization posters

ARMÉE DE TERRE ET ARMÉE DE MER

ORDRE DE MOBILISATION GÉNÉRALE

Par décret du Président de la République, la mobilisation des armées de terre et de mer est ordonnée, ainsi que la réquisition des animaux, voitures et harnais nécessaires au complément de ces armées.

Le premier jour de la mobilisation est le Dimanche deux Août 1914

Tout Français soumis aux obligations militaires doit, sous peine d'être puni avec toute rigueur des lois, obéir aux prescriptions du FASCICULE DE MOBILISATION (pages colorées placées dans son livret).

Sont visés par le présent ordre TOUS LES HOMMES non présents sous les Drapeaux et appartenant :

1° à l'ARMÉE DE TERRE y compris les TROUPES COLONIALES et les hommes des SERVICES AUXILIAIRES;

2° à l'ARMÉE DE MER y compris les INSCRITS MARITIMES et les ARMÉES de la MARINE.

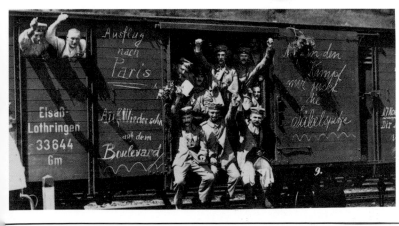

Vive La France
The French army mobilized on 1 August. For many Frenchmen, the war was a chance to seek revenge for the German defeat of France in 1870–71.

All aboard!
The German troops on this westbound train believed that the offensive against France would soon take them to Paris. French troops felt the same about Berlin.

> *"The lamps are going out all over Europe."*
>
> *SIR EDWARD GREY*
> *BRITISH FOREIGN SECRETARY, 1914*

war; France mobilizes in support of its ally, Russia; Germany signs a treaty with Ottoman Turkey; Italy declares its neutrality	**2 August** Germany invades Luxemburg **3 August** Germany declares war on France	**4 August** Germany invades Belgium on route to France; Britain enters the war to safeguard Belgian neutrality	**6 August** Austria-Hungary declares war on Russia **12 August** France and Britain declare war on Austria-Hungary

Christmas treat
The City of London Territorial Association sent each of its soldiers a tinned plum pudding for Christmas in 1914.

War in the west

By 1905, fearing war on two fronts, Germany's Field Marshal Count Alfred von Schlieffen had developed a plan to knock France swiftly out of any war before turning against Russia. In August 1914, the plan went into operation. German troops crossed the Belgian border on 4 August, and by the end of the month, invaded northern France. At the Battle of the Marne on 5 September, the German advance was held and pushed back. By Christmas 1914, the two sides faced stalemate on the Western Front, along a line from the Belgian coast in the north to the Swiss border in the south.

In retreat
Unable to block the German army, Belgian soldiers with dog-drawn machine guns withdraw to Antwerp.

In the field
The British Expeditionary Force (B.E.F.) had arrived in France by 22 August 1914. Its cavalry division included members of the Royal Horse Artillery, whose L Battery fired this 13-pounder quick-firing Mark I gun against the German 4th Cavalry Division at the Battle of Néry on 1 September.

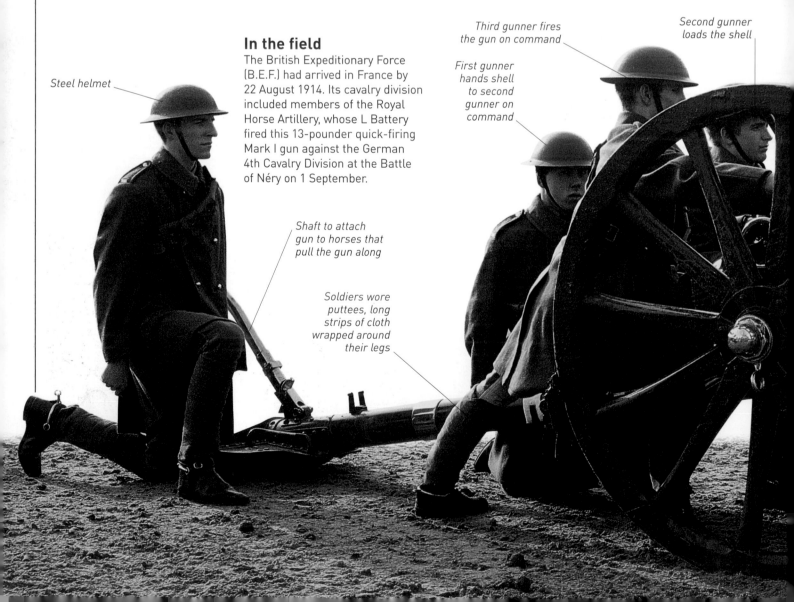

Steel helmet

Shaft to attach gun to horses that pull the gun along

Soldiers wore puttees, long strips of cloth wrapped around their legs

Third gunner fires the gun on command

First gunner hands shell to second gunner on command

Second gunner loads the shell

The Christmas truce

On Christmas Eve 1914, soldiers on both sides of the Western Front sang carols to each other. The next day, troops along two-thirds of the front observed a truce. All firing stopped, and church services were held. A few soldiers crossed into no-man's-land to talk to their enemy and exchange cigarettes and other gifts. South of Ypres, Belgium, the two sides even played a game of football. One year later, however, sentries on both sides were ordered to shoot anyone attempting a repeat performance.

Eyewitness
Captain E.R.P. Berryman wrote a letter home describing the truce. This cartoon illustrates the absurdity of his situation – shooting the enemy one day and greeting them as friends the next.

British soldier shooting at enemy with a note saying "Christmas Eve – Get 'em!"

British and German soldiers greeting each other on Christmas Day

German trench

Rope wrapped around recoil mechanism

Fires 5.6-kg (12.5-lb) shells a distance of 5,395 m (17,700 ft)

Heading for the front
By early September, German troops were only 40 km (25 miles) east of Paris. The city's military governor used 600 taxis to take 6,000 men to reinforce the front line.

Fighting men

The outbreak of war in August 1914 changed the lives of millions. Regular soldiers, older reservists, eager recruits, and unwilling conscripts were all caught up in the war. Some were experienced soldiers, but many had barely held a rifle before. Britain and France also drew heavily on armies recruited from their empires.

France

Hat flaps could be pulled down to keep out the cold

Ammunition pouch

Winter jerkin made of goat- or sheepskin

Grand Duke Nicholas

In 1914, the Russian army was led by the Tsar's uncle, Grand Duke Nicholas. As commander-in-chief, he dealt with the overall strategy of the war, and his generals directed the battles. The other warring countries had similar chains of command.

The British army

At the start of war, the British army contained just 247,432 regulars and 218,280 reservists. They wore a khaki uniform consisting of a single-breasted tunic, trousers, puttees or leggings worn to protect the shins, and ankleboots.

Woollen puttees wrapped around shins

British soldier

Lee Enfield rifle No. 1 MkIII

Thick boots to protect feet

Russia

Empire troops

Britain and France drew on their colonies in Africa, Asia, the Pacific, and the Caribbean for large numbers of recruits. The British dominions of Australia, New Zealand, Canada, and South Africa also sent their armies to take part in the conflict. Many of these men had never left home before. The Annamites (Indo-Chinese) above, from French Indo-China, were stationed at Salonika, Greece, in 1916.

Eastern allies

In Eastern Europe, Germany faced the vast Russian army, as well as smaller armies from Serbia and Montenegro. In the Far East, German colonies in China and the Pacific Ocean were invaded by Japan.

France

Britain

Belgium

Western allies

In Western Europe, Britain, France, and Belgium were allied against Germany. Unlike the British and French armies, the Belgian army was small and inexperienced.

French infantrymen photographed in 1918

The French army

Including reservists and colonial troops, the French army totalled 3,680,000 trained men at the outbreak of war.

Steel helmets were issued in 1916

Field tunic (Waffenrock)

Tent cloth

Cartridge pouch

Mauser rifle

Water bottle

Haversack with personal items

Lebel rifle

Stick grenade

French infantryman, known as *le poilu*

Gas mask

German soldier

The German army

In 1914, the German army was the strongest in Europe, with 840,000 men. All men under the age of 45 were trained for military service and belonged to the reserve army. On calling up the reserves, the German army could expand to more than four million trained men.

Russia

Serbia

Montenegro

Japan

Joining up

At the outbreak of war, unlike Europe's large armies of conscripts, Britain had only a small army made up of volunteers. On 6 August 1914, the Secretary of War, Lord Kitchener, asked for 100,000 new recruits. Whole streets and villages of patriotic men queued to enlist.

War leader
Britain's prime minister in 1914 Herbert Asquith, was known as "the last of the Romans".

The test
Every British recruit had a medical test to make sure he was fit to fight. Many failed the test, because of poor eyesight or ill health. Others were refused because they were under 19, although many lied about their age.

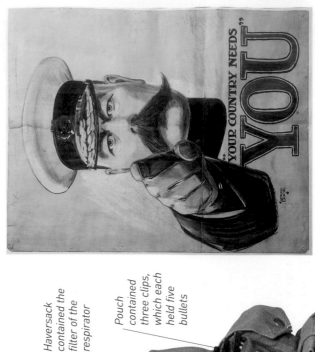

"Your country needs you"
A portrait of Lord Kitchener was used as a recruiting poster in 1914. Some 2,446,719 men had enlisted by1916, but more were needed.

Small box respirator gas mask

Haversack contained the filter of the respirator

Pouch contained three clips, which each held five bullets

Two sets of five ammunition pouches on belt

Queue here for king and country
At the outbreak of war, men from the same area or industry joined Pals battalions, so they could fight together. By mid-September, half a million men had volunteered.

On les aura!

2ᴱ EMPRUNT DE **LA DÉFENSE NATIONALE** Souscrivez

DEVAMBEZ IMP. PARIS

Tin for tea and stock cubes

Linen bag to store iron ration

Tin of bully beef

Biscuits

BISCUITS LB.

Rations

Each soldier was given an emergency "iron ration", in case he was cut off from the daily supply of food. It included hard biscuits, corned beef, tea, and stock cubes.

Haversack used for soldier's kit when in the trenches

Bayonet

Entrenching tool handle

Holdall

Razor case

Boot laces

Water-bottle

Knife

Cut-throat razor

Shaving brush

Fork

Spoon

Button stick

RAZOR

RB 2600

Soldier's small kit

The basic kit

A British soldier carried enough basic equipment to fight and to survive in the trenches: his rifle and bayonet, ammunition, and an entrenching tool to dig a shallow hole to take cover in. By 1917, he also carried a respirator in case of gas attacks. His survival kit included cutlery, a washing kit, and spare clothes. Going into battle, he put the most needed items into a smaller haversack.

Conscientious objectors

Some people who refused to join up were given white feathers as a sign of cowardice. Certain religious groups objected to the war because they believed it was wrong to kill, and some Socialists objected to fighting fellow workers. Both groups were known as conscientious objectors. Some objectors served in non-combatant units, such as medical services.

Paying for the troops

The cost of raising and supplying armies meant each country had to raise taxes. Banks and private investors were asked to lend money to their government in the form of war loans. This French poster crums up support with the words 'On les aura!' ("We'll get them!").

Empire troops

When war was declared, thousands of men volunteered from across the British Empire. New recruits augmented existing regiments, such as these Bengal Lancers. Indian troops served with distinction, far from home.

Stalemate

At the outbreak of war, both sides on the Western Front were equipped with powerful, long-range artillery weapons and rapid-fire machine guns. These weapons made it dangerous for soldiers to fight in unprotected, open ground. So they dug defensive trenches, and found themselves trapped in a static fight.

Blade cover

— Front line of trenches

The front line
By December 1914, a network of trenches ran along the Western Front from the Belgian coast in the north down through eastern France to the Swiss border, 645 km (400 miles) in the south.

The first trenches
Early trenches were just deep furrows, providing minimal cover from enemy fire. Troops from the 2nd Scots Guards dug this trench near Ypres, Belgium, in October 1914.

Entrenching tools
Each soldier carried an entrenching tool. He used it to dig a scrape – a shallow trench – if he was caught out in the open by enemy fire. He could also use it to repair a trench damaged by an enemy artillery bombardment.

American M1910 entrenching tool

Signposts
Each trench was signposted, often with its nickname, to avoid soldiers losing their way.

Positioning the trench
The Gemans usually built trenches where they could best observe and fire at the enemy while remaining concealed. The British and French preferred to capture as much ground as possible before digging their trenches.

Boarded up

By summer 1915, many German trenches were reinforced with wooden walls to prevent them from collapsing onto the troops and burying them alive. They were also dug very deep to help protect the men from artillery bombardments.

Home sweet home?

The Germans constructed the most elaborate trenches, regarding them as the new German border. Many trenches had shuttered windows and even doormats to wipe muddy boots on!

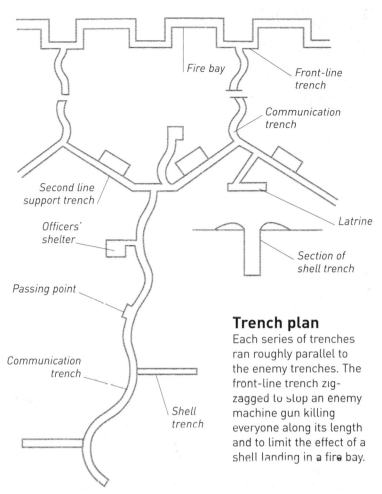

Trench plan

Each series of trenches ran roughly parallel to the enemy trenches. The front-line trench zig-zagged to stop an enemy machine gun killing everyone along its length and to limit the effect of a shell landing in a fire bay.

Coping with the mud

Rain, snow, and natural seepage soon filled trenches with water. Wooden slats, known as duckboards, were laid on the ground to keep soldiers' feet reasonably dry, but it was always muddy.

Life in the trenches

Most of the work in the trenches was done at night when patrols were sent out to observe and raid enemy trenches, and to repair their own defences. Dawn and dusk were the most likely times for an enemy attack, so all the troops "stood to", that is manned the fire bays, at these times. The days were usually quiet. To relieve the boredom, soldiers spent one week to ten days in the front line, then moved into the reserve lines, and finally went to the rear to rest. Here, they were given a bath and freshly laundered clothes before returning to the trenches.

A little shelter
The trenches were usually very narrow and often exposed to the weather. These Canadian soldiers have built a makeshift canopy to shelter under.

Soldier removing mud from ammunition pouch with a piece of cloth

A relaxing read?
This reconstruction from London's Imperial War Museum shows a soldier reading to while away the long hours of waiting.

Clean and tidy
Waterproofing boots and cleaning kit was as much a part of life in the trenches as it was in the barracks back home. These Belgian soldiers cleaning their rifles knew that such tasks were essential to maintaining combat efficiency.

Officers' dug-out
This re-creation in London's Imperial War Museum of an officers' dug-out on the Somme in autumn 1916 shows the cramped conditions people endured in the trenches. The officer on the telephone is calling in artillery support for an imminent trench raid, while his weary comrade is asleep behind him on a camp bed.

The French author Henri Barbusse wrote of trench life in his anti-war novel *Le Feu (Under Fire)* of 1916

Artists and poets

Some soldiers in the trenches wrote poems or made sketches. Many wrote long letters home, or kept a diary. These records of trench life make fascinating and shocking reading. In 1916, the British government began to send official war artists, such as Paul Nash, to the front to record the war in paint.

The Menin Road (1918) by British war artist Paul Nash

Poem and self-portrait by the British poet and artist Isaac Rosenberg

Paints and brushes belonging to Paul Nash

Cave men

Ordinary soldiers – such as these British troops at Thiepval Wood on the Somme in 1916 – spent their time off duty in "funk holes", carved out of the side of the trench, or under waterproof sheets.

Trench cuisine

These French officers are dining well in a reserve trench. Others ate tinned food or mass-produced meals brought up from behind the lines and reheated in the trench.

Rats and lice infested the trenches

Ready to fight

Soldiers on the Western Front rarely left their trenches to fight in open ground, or no-man's-land, between the two opposing front lines. But there was a constant battle between soldiers in their facing lines of trenches. Both armies shot at anyone who was visible on the other side, even those trying to rescue the wounded from no-man's-land or retrieve bodies caught on the barbed-wire fences. Raiding parties added to the danger. Every soldier was kept on full alert.

Prepare to fire

These German troops on the Marne in 1914 are firing through gun holes. These enabled them to view and fire at the enemy without putting their heads above the parapet and exposing themselves to enemy fire. Later on in the war, sandbags replaced the earth ramparts.

At close quarters

Soldiers carried a range of close-combat weapons when they went on raiding parties, in case they needed to kill an enemy silently, without being detected.

Writing home

Both armies had chaplains and other clergy at the front. As a non-combatant, Canon Cyril Lomax had time to describe in illustrated letters home some of the horrors he encountered.

French trench knife

German stick grenade

German club

German timed and fused ball grenade

British Mills bomb

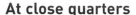

Walking wounded

This reconstruction in London's Imperial War Museum shows a British medical orderly escorting a wounded German prisoner from the front line through the trench system to a an aid post. A soldier wounded in no-man's-land would be left until it was safe to bring him back to his trench, usually at nightfall. Some soldiers died because they could not be reached soon enough.

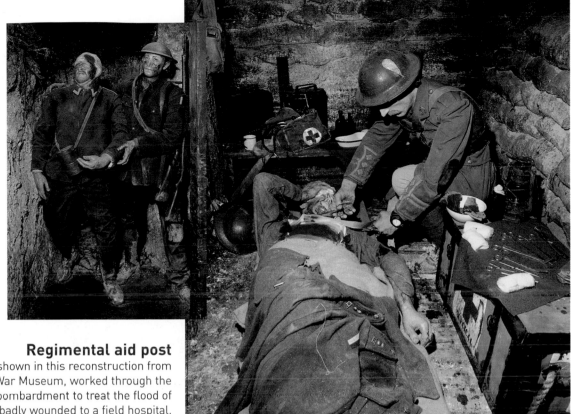

Regimental aid post

Medical officers, as shown in this reconstruction from London's Imperial War Museum, worked through the heat of battle and bombardment to treat the flood of casualties and sent the badly wounded to a field hospital.

Path of bullet

Always in action

These Bulgarian soldiers are eating in shifts. In the trenches a look-out had to be kept 24 hours a day, with guns always primed and ready, in case the enemy mounted a sudden attack.

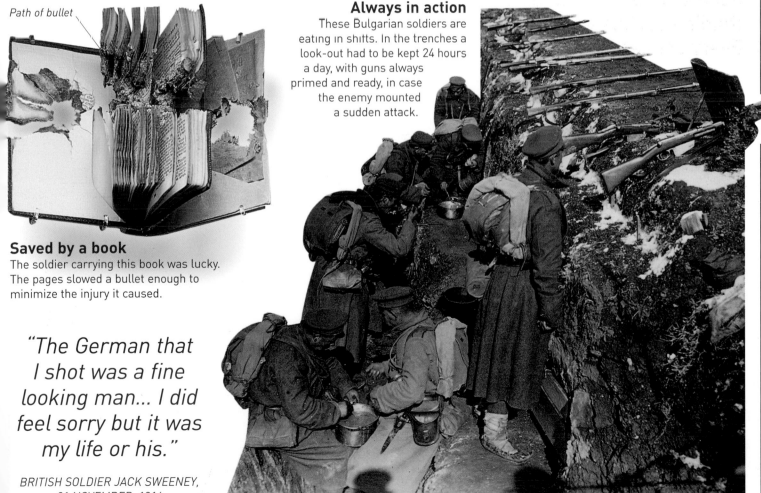

Saved by a book

The soldier carrying this book was lucky. The pages slowed a bullet enough to minimize the injury it caused.

"The German that I shot was a fine looking man... I did feel sorry but it was my life or his."

BRITISH SOLDIER JACK SWEENEY, 21 NOVEMBER, 1916

Communication

To supply the vast and hungry armies along the Western Front, both sides put huge effort into lines of communication. The main form of transport was the horse and, increasingly, motor vehicles. Germany made great use of railways to move men and supplies to the front. Both sides set up elaborate supply systems to ensure that front-line troops never ran out of munitions or food. Front-line troops also kept in close touch with headquarters and other units by telephone and wireless.

Field telephone
Most communication was by telephones relaying voice and Morse code messages.

British night signal

Getting in touch
Engineers, such as this German team, set up, maintained, and operated telephones in the field, to ensure close and regular contact between the front line and HQ.

Missile messages
Enemy fire often cut telephone lines, so both sides used shells to carry written messages. Signal grenades and rockets also sent pre-arranged messages to front-line troops.

Message rolled up in base

German message shell

French army pigeon handler's badge

Canvas top secured with ropes

LOAD NOT TO EXCEED 3 TONS

WD

Pigeon post
Carrier pigeons were used to carry messages to and from the front line where telephone lines did not exist, although the birds often lost their way. Germany trained "war dogs" to carry messages in containers on their collars.

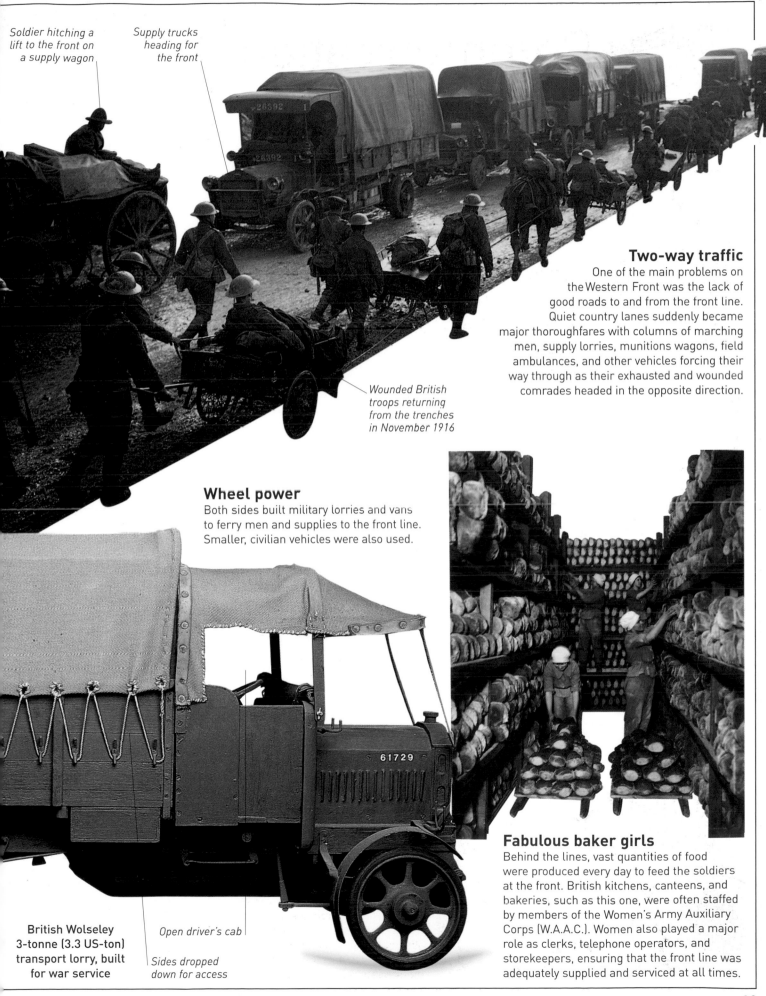

*Soldier hitching a
lift to the front on
a supply wagon*

*Supply trucks
heading for
the front*

Two-way traffic

One of the main problems on
the Western Front was the lack of
good roads to and from the front line.
Quiet country lanes suddenly became
major thoroughfares with columns of marching
men, supply lorries, munitions wagons, field
ambulances, and other vehicles forcing their
way through as their exhausted and wounded
comrades headed in the opposite direction.

*Wounded British
troops returning
from the trenches
in November 1916*

Wheel power

Both sides built military lorries and vans
to ferry men and supplies to the front line.
Smaller, civilian vehicles were also used.

61729

Fabulous baker girls

Behind the lines, vast quantities of food
were produced every day to feed the soldiers
at the front. British kitchens, canteens, and
bakeries, such as this one, were often staffed
by members of the Women's Army Auxiliary
Corps (W.A.A.C.). Women also played a major
role as clerks, telephone operators, and
storekeepers, ensuring that the front line was
adequately supplied and serviced at all times.

*British Wolseley
3-tonne (3.3 US-ton)
transport lorry, built
for war service*

Open driver's cab

*Sides dropped
down for access*

Keeping watch

Gathering intelligence about the enemy is vital to mounting a successful attack or repelling an enemy advance. As in every war, prisoners were interrogated. Night-time patrols probed the strengths and weaknesses of enemy lines, crossing rows of barbed-wire entanglements and running the risk of disturbing unexploded shells or attracting enemy gunfire. Aircraft flew virtually unhindered over the enemy to observe their trenches and gun emplacements and to photograph the front line. This information was used to produce maps of enemy lines.

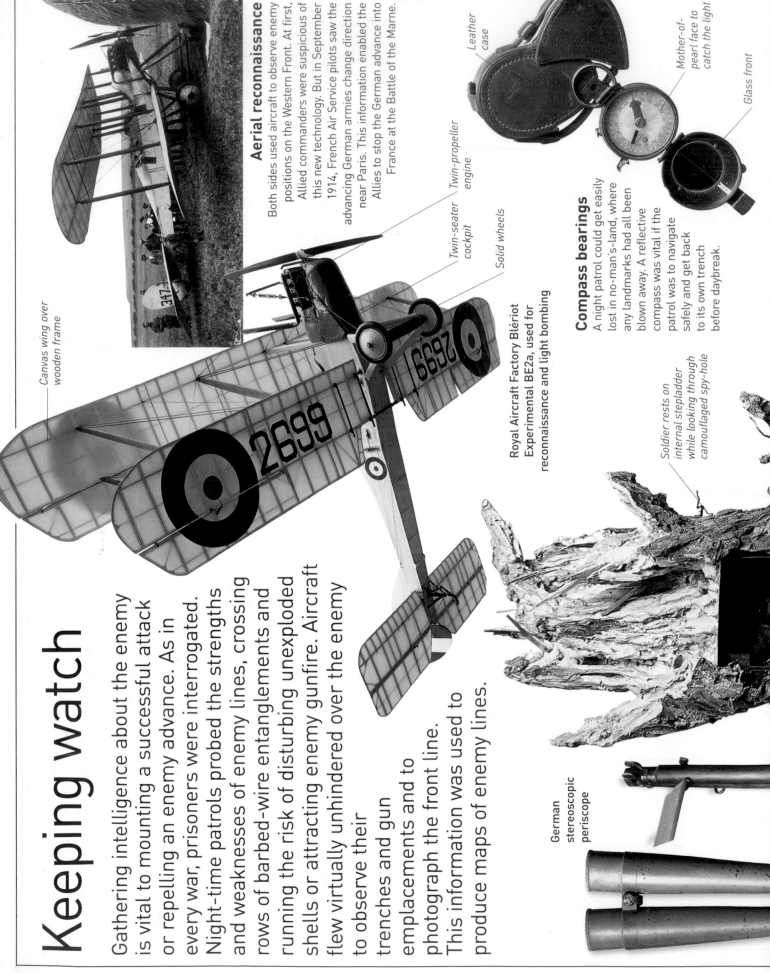

Canvas wing over wooden frame

Aerial reconnaissance

Both sides used aircraft to observe enemy positions on the Western Front. At first, Allied commanders were suspicious of this new technology. But in September 1914, French Air Service pilots saw the advancing German armies change direction near Paris. This information enabled the Allies to stop the German advance into France at the Battle of the Marne.

Twin-propeller engine

Twin-seater cockpit

Solid wheels

Royal Aircraft Factory Blériot Experimental BE2a, used for reconnaissance and light bombing

Leather case

Mother-of-pearl face to catch the light

Glass front

Compass bearings

A night patrol could get easily lost in no-man's-land, where any landmarks had all been blown away. A reflective compass was vital if the patrol was to navigate safely and get back to its own trench before daybreak.

Soldier rests on internal stepladder while looking through camouflaged spy-hole

German stereoscopic periscope

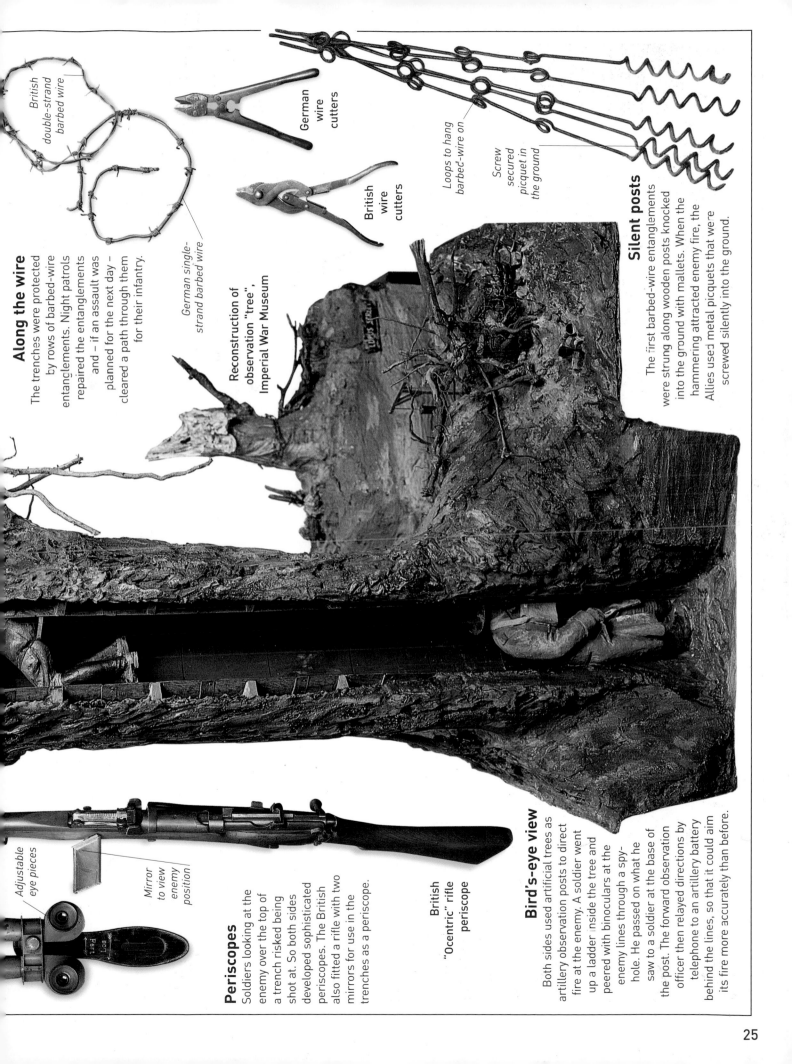

British double-strand barbed wire

Along the wire

The trenches were protected by rows of barbed-wire entanglements. Night patrols repaired the entanglements and – if an assault was planned for the next day – cleared a path through them for their infantry.

German wire cutters

British wire cutters

German single-strand barbed wire

Loops to hang barbed-wire on

Screw secured picquet in the ground

Silent posts

The first barbed-wire entanglements were strung along wooden posts knocked into the ground with mallets. When the hammering attracted enemy fire, the Allies used metal picquets that were screwed silently into the ground.

Reconstruction of observation "tree", Imperial War Museum

Bird's-eye view

Both sides used artificial trees as artillery observation posts to direct fire at the enemy. A soldier went up a ladder inside the tree and peered with binoculars at the enemy lines through a spy-hole. He passed on what he saw to a soldier at the base of the post. The forward observation officer then relayed directions by telephone to an artillery battery behind the lines, so that it could aim its fire more accurately than before.

British "Ocentric" rifle periscope

Periscopes

Soldiers looking at the enemy over the top of a trench risked being shot at. So both sides developed sophisticated periscopes. The British also fitted a rifle with two mirrors for use in the trenches as a periscope.

Adjustable eye pieces

Mirror to view enemy position

Bombardment

Sight saver
A chain-mail visor on British helmets made it hard to see and was soon removed.

Beware!
Soldiers at the front needed constant reminders to keep their heads down.

Artillery dominated the battlefields of World War I. A bombardment could destroy enemy trenches, knock out artillery batteries and communication lines, and help break up an infantry attack. As defences strengthened, artillery bombardments became longer and more intense.

Helmet

German armour
In 1916, the German army replaced its spiked *Pickelhaube* helmet with a rounded, steel helmet and issued body armour to machine gunners.

Visor

Breastplate

Articulated plates to cover lower body

Hiding the gun
Light field artillery was pulled by horses, while heavier guns, such as howitzers, were moved by tractors. Once in place, artillery pieces were camouflaged.

British 20-cm (8-in) Mark V howitzer

Shell power
A huge number of shells was needed to maintain a constant artillery barrage. In mid-1917, the British used a million shells a day.

Loading a howitzer

Large pieces of artillery required a team of experienced gunners to load and fire them. This British 38-cm (15-in) howitzer was used on the Menin Road near Ypres in October 1917. Its huge, heavy shell is being winched into position.

Explosion!

In this dramatic picture, a British tank has just been hit by a high-explosive shell. To its right, another tank breaks through the barbed wire. It was unusual for moving targets such as tanks to be hit. Most artillery fire was used to soften up the enemy lines before an attack.

British 5.9-kg (13-lb) high-explosive shell

French 75-mm (2.9-in) shrapnel shell

British 11.4-cm (4.5-in) high-explosive shell

German 15-cm (5.9-in) shrapnel shell

Artillery shells

High-explosive shells exploded on impact. Anti-personnel shrapnel shells exploded in flight, designed to kill or maim.

Over the top

Once the artillery bombardment had pounded the enemy's defences, the infantry climbed out of their trenches and advanced towards enemy lines. But artillery bombardments rarely knocked out every enemy defence, and gaps were filled by highly mobile machine-gunners. A soldier armed with only a rifle and bayonet and laden with heavy equipment was an easy target.

Leaving the trench
The most frightening moment for a soldier was climbing out of his trench and into no-man's-land.

Steel water jacket to cool gun barrel

Disc is part of the flash hider assembly, making the gun harder to spot

German MG '08 Maxim machine gun

Trench mounting

In action
This German machine-gun crew protects the flank (side) of advancing infantry. The manoeuvrability, reliability, and firepower of machine guns made them effective weapons and difficult for the enemy to destroy.

British 7.7-mm (0.303-in) Maxim Mark 3 medium machine gun

Water-cooled barrel

Quick firing
Machine guns fired up to 600 bullets a minute. Ammunition was fitted into a belt, or in a tray fed into the gun automatically.

Tripod mounting

Futile attack

The Battle of the Somme in France lasted from 1 July 1916 until 18 November, when snow and rain brought the attack to a muddy halt. The Allies took about 125 sq km (48 sq miles) of land, but failed to break through the German lines north of the River Somme.

"The sunken road... (was)... filled with pieces of uniform, weapons, and dead bodies."

LIEUTENANT ERNST JUNGER, GERMAN SOLDIER, THE SOMME, 1916

First day on the Somme

The British began a six-day artillery bombardment on 24 June, but the Germans retreated into deep bunkers and were largely unharmed. As the British infantry advanced at 7.30 am on 1 July, German machine gunners opened fire. On that first day alone, they killed or injured two British soldiers along each metre (three feet) of the 25-km (16-mile) front.

Soldiers of the 103rd (Tyneside Irish) Brigade attack La Boisselle on the first day of the Somme

Tending the wounded

The cramped conditions in a muddy trench can be seen in this image of an army medical officer tending a wounded soldier at Thiepval near the Somme in September 1916.

Casualty

An estimated 21 million soldiers were wounded in the war. Caring for casualties was a major military operation. They were first treated in the trenches, then moved to casualty clearing stations behind the front line for proper medical attention, then on to base hospitals still further from the front. Soldiers with severe injuries went home to recover in hospitals.

Lucky man
When a splinter from a shell pierced his helmet, this soldier escaped with only a minor head wound. Many received severe injuries that stayed with them for life.

Trench aid
Injured soldiers had their wounds dressed by medical orderlies in the trench where they fell, before being taken to an aid post for assessment.

Strip of lace curtain

Recycled bandages
Following the naval blockade by Britain, Germany ran out of cotton and linen. Wood fibre, paper, and lace curtains were used to make bandages.

German bandages

Inventory listing contents and where to find them in the pouch

Bottles of liquid antiseptics and painkillers

The German kit
German medical orderlies carried two first-aid pouches on their belts. One contained basic antiseptics and painkillers, while the other contained dressings and triangular bandages.

Forceps and clamps held securely in a metal tray

Lower tray contains saws and knives for amputation

Tools of the trade

Army doctors carried a standard set of surgical instruments. They faced a wide variety of injuries, from bullets and shell fragments.

The field hospital

Farmhouses, ruined factories, and even bombed-out churches, were used as casualty clearing stations to treat the wounded.

Shellshock

Shellshock – the collective term for concussion, emotional shock, nervous exhaustion, and similar ailments – was not identified before World War I, but trench warfare was so horrific that large numbers of soldiers developed symptoms. Most eventually recovered, but some suffered nightmares and other effects for the rest of their lives.

A medical orderly helps a wounded soldier away from the trenches

Bunks for the injured to lie on

Ambulance

The British Royal Army Medical Corps, like its German counterpart, used field ambulances to carry the wounded to hospital. Many ambulances were staffed by volunteers, often women.

Red Cross symbol to signify non-combatant status of the ambulance

Women at war

When the men went off to fight, the women had to take their place. Many women were already in work but were restricted to domestic labour, nursing, teaching, or working on the family farm – jobs considered suitable for women. Now they went to work in factories, drove trucks and ambulances, and did almost everything that only men had done before. When the war ended, most women returned to the home.

Front-line adventure
British nurse Elsie Knocker (above) went to Belgium in 1914 where she and Mairi Chisholm set up a dressing station at Pervyse. They were almost the only women on the front line, dressing the wounded until both were gassed in 1918.

Army laundry
Traditional women's work, such as working in a laundry or bakery, continued during the war on a huge scale. This British Army laundry in France cleaned the clothes of thousands of soldiers every day.

Women's Army Auxillary Corps
Many women were enlisted into auxiliary armies to release the men for the front line. They drove trucks, mended engines, and did much of the vital administration and supply work. In Britain, the recruitment poster for The Women's (later Queen Mary's) Army Auxiliary Corps described a khaki-clad woman (left) as "The girl behind the man behind the gun".

Women's Land Army

The war required a huge increase in food production at home as both sides tried to restrict the enemy's imports of food from abroad. In Britain, 113,000 women joined the Women's Land Army, set up in February 1917 to provide a well-paid female workforce to run the farms. Millions of women already worked the land across Europe.

Support your country

Images of "ideal" women were used to gain support for a country's war effort. This Russian poster urges people to buy war bonds (loans to the government).

Russia's amazons

A number of Russian women joined the "Legion of Death" to fight – and in many cases to die – for their country.

Letters to men at the front describing events at home

Family photographs

Lace handkerchief

Working in poverty

The war brought increased status and wealth to many women, but not all. In factories across Italy (above), Germany, and Russia, women worked long, hard hours but earned barely enough to feed their families. Strikes led by women were very common as a result.

Mementos from home

Women wrote letters to their husbands, brothers, and sons at the front. They often enclosed keepsakes, such as photographs or pressed flowers, to remind them of home. These did much to raise the morale of homesick and often very frightened men.

War in the air

Dogfights
Guns were mounted on top of aircraft, so pilots had to fly straight at the enemy to shoot.

When war broke out in 1914, the history of powered flight was barely ten years old. The first warplanes flew as reconnaissance craft, looking down on enemy lines or helping to direct artillery fire. Enemy pilots tried to shoot them down, leading to dogfights in the sky between highly skilled and brave "aces". Specialized fighter planes were soon produced by both sides, as were sturdier craft capable of carrying bombs.

Leather face mask

Leather balaclava

Turned-up collar to keep neck warm

Anti-splinter glass goggles

Pouch for maps

Coat of soft, supple leather

Sheepskin-lined leather gloves to protect against frostbite

Sopwith Camel
The Sopwith F1 Camel first flew in battle in June 1917 and became the most successful Allied fighter in shooting down German aircraft.

Wooden, box-structure wings covered with canvas

8.2-m (26.9-ft) wingspan

Propeller to guide the bomb

Dressed for the air
Pilots flew in open cockpits, so they wore leather coats, balaclavas, and boots and gloves lined with sheepskin to keep out the cold. One-piece suits also became common.

Thick sole to give a good grip

Sheepskin boots

Bombs away
At first, bombs were dropped over the side of the aircraft by the pilot. Soon, specialized bomber aircraft were fitted with bombsights, bomb racks under the fuselage, and release systems.

British 9.1-kg (20-lb) Marten Hale bomb, containing 2 kg (4.5 lb) of explosives

Fins to stop the bomb from spinning on its descent

Perforated casing to help bomb catch fire on impact

British Carcass incendiary bomb

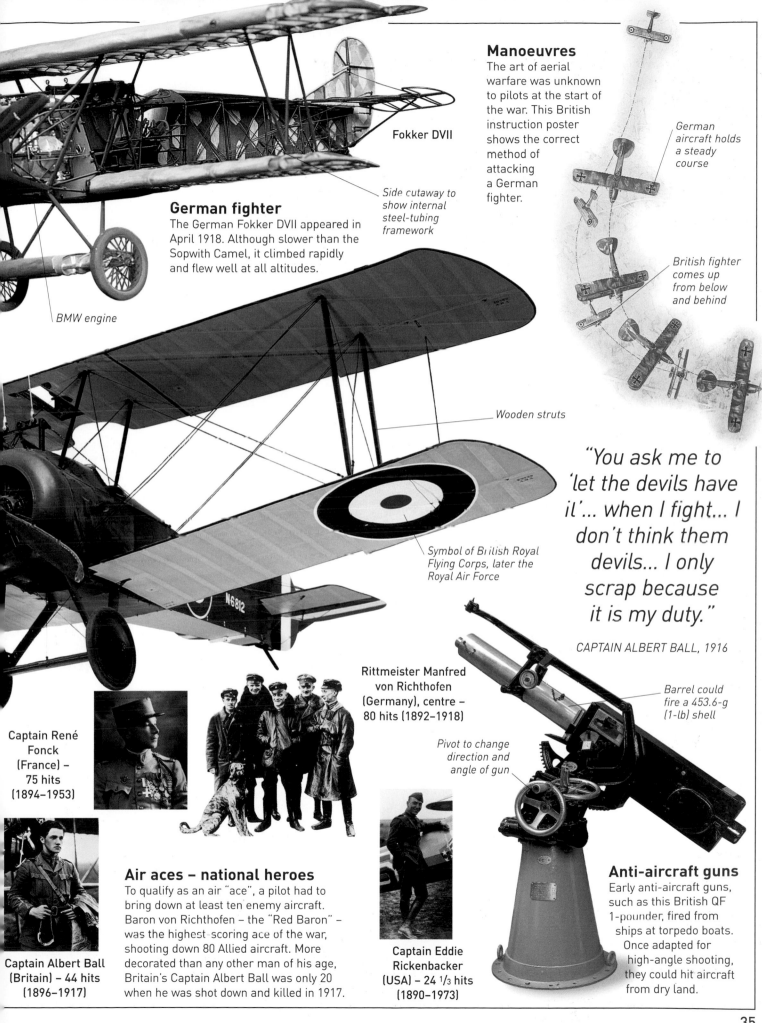

Fokker DVII

German fighter
The German Fokker DVII appeared in April 1918. Although slower than the Sopwith Camel, it climbed rapidly and flew well at all altitudes.

Side cutaway to show internal steel-tubing framework

BMW engine

Manoeuvres
The art of aerial warfare was unknown to pilots at the start of the war. This British instruction poster shows the correct method of attacking a German fighter.

German aircraft holds a steady course

British fighter comes up from below and behind

Wooden struts

Symbol of British Royal Flying Corps, later the Royal Air Force

N6812

"You ask me to 'let the devils have it'... when I fight... I don't think them devils... I only scrap because it is my duty."

CAPTAIN ALBERT BALL, 1916

Barrel could fire a 453.6-g (1-lb) shell

Rittmeister Manfred von Richthofen (Germany), centre – 80 hits (1892–1918)

Captain René Fonck (France) – 75 hits (1894–1953)

Pivot to change direction and angle of gun

Air aces – national heroes
To qualify as an air "ace", a pilot had to bring down at least ten enemy aircraft. Baron von Richthofen – the "Red Baron" – was the highest-scoring ace of the war, shooting down 80 Allied aircraft. More decorated than any other man of his age, Britain's Captain Albert Ball was only 20 when he was shot down and killed in 1917.

Captain Albert Ball (Britain) – 44 hits (1896–1917)

Captain Eddie Rickenbacker (USA) – 24 1/3 hits (1890–1973)

Anti-aircraft guns
Early anti-aircraft guns, such as this British QF 1-pounder, fired from ships at torpedo boats. Once adapted for high-angle shooting, they could hit aircraft from dry land.

Zeppelin

The first airship was designed by the German Count Ferdinand von Zeppelin in 1900. Early in the war, airships could fly higher than planes, so it was almost impossible to shoot them down. This made them useful for carrying out bombing raids. But higher flying aircraft and the use of incendiary (fire-making) bullets soon brought these aerial bombers down to earth. By 1917, most German and British airships were restricted to reconnaissance work at sea.

Fuel tank

Gondola

Bombs away!
Crews in the first airships had to drop their bombs over the side of the gondola by hand. Later models had automatic release mechanisms.

Inside the gondola
Exposed to the weather, the crew operated the airship from the open-sided gondola – a cabin below the main airship.

German incendiary bomb dropped by Zeppelin LZ38 on London, 31 May 1915

Getting bigger
This L3 German airship took part in the first airship raid on Britain on the night of 19–20 January 1915, causing 20 civilian casualties and enormous panic.

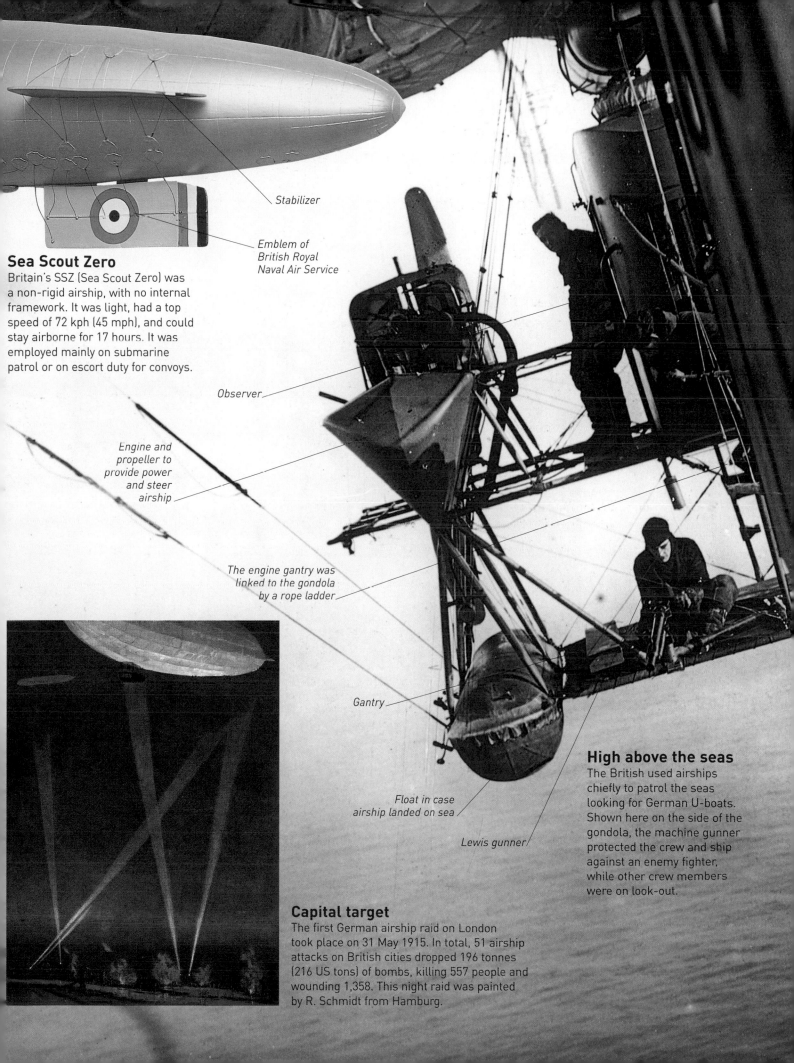

Sea Scout Zero

Britain's SSZ (Sea Scout Zero) was a non-rigid airship, with no internal framework. It was light, had a top speed of 72 kph (45 mph), and could stay airborne for 17 hours. It was employed mainly on submarine patrol or on escort duty for convoys.

Stabilizer

Emblem of British Royal Naval Air Service

Observer

Engine and propeller to provide power and steer airship

The engine gantry was linked to the gondola by a rope ladder

Gantry

Float in case airship landed on sea

Lewis gunner

High above the seas

The British used airships chiefly to patrol the seas looking for German U-boats. Shown here on the side of the gondola, the machine gunner protected the crew and ship against an enemy fighter, while other crew members were on look-out.

Capital target

The first German airship raid on London took place on 31 May 1915. In total, 51 airship attacks on British cities dropped 196 tonnes (216 US tons) of bombs, killing 557 people and wounding 1,358. This night raid was painted by R. Schmidt from Hamburg.

War at sea

The war was fought largely on land, with both sides avoiding naval conflict. The British fleet had to keep the seas open for merchant ships bringing food and other supplies to Britain, and prevent supplies reaching Germany. Germany needed its fleet to protect itself against possible invasion. The main fight took place under the sea, as German U-boats attacked Allied ships.

"I want you"
When the USA entered the war in April 1917, a recruiting poster had this attractive woman in naval uniform.

Constant threat
This German poster, *The U-boats are out!*, shows the threat posed to Allied shipping by the German U-boat fleet.

Life inside a U-boat
Conditions inside a U-boat were cramped, and fumes and heat from the engine made the air very stuffy. The crew had to navigate their craft through minefields and avoid detection in order to attack enemy ships.

Land and sea
Seaplanes can take off and land on both water and the ground. Used for reconnaissance and bombing, they could sink an enemy ship with a torpedo.

Floats for landing on water

Observation balloon

Gun

Success and failure
German U-boats operated under the sea and on the surface. Here, a deck cannon fires at an enemy steamer. The U-boats sank 5,554 Allied and neutral merchant ships as well as many warships. But 178 of the 372 U-boats were destroyed by Allied bombs or torpedoes.

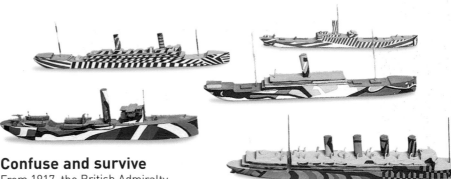

Confuse and survive
From 1917, the British Admiralty camouflaged merchant ships and their escorts with grey, black, and blue geometric patterns. This distorted the silhouette of the ship and made it difficult for German U-boats to target.

Dazzled
Many artists contributed to their country's war effort, some in surprising ways. The British painter Edward Wadsworth supervised the application of "dazzle" camouflage to ships' hulls. He later painted the picture above, *Dazzle ships in dry dock at Liverpool*, showing the finished result.

Medals awarded to Jack Cornwall

Victoria Cross (VC)

British War Medal

Victory Medal

Boy at the Battle of Jutland
John Travers Cornwall was only 16 when he first saw action at Jutland, the war's only major sea battle, on 31 May 1916. Mortally wounded, he stayed at his post until the end of the action.

The British Grand Fleet
Britain's Royal Navy was the biggest in the world and followed the "two-power standard" – its might equalled that of the two next strongest nations combined. Despite this superiority, the navy played a more limited role in the war compared with the army, keeping the seas free of German ships and escorting merchant convoys.

Flight deck

HMS *Furious*
Aircraft carriers first saw service in World War I. On 7 July 1918, seven Sopwith Camels took off from HMS *Furious* to attack a zeppelin base at Tondern in northern Germany.

Gallipoli

In 1915, the Allies tried to force through the Dardanelles Strait and take the Ottoman Turkish capital, Constantinople. Two attacks failed. On 25 April, British, Australian, and New Zealand troops landed on the Gallipoli peninsula. In August, there was a second landing on the peninsula, at Suvla Bay, but the Allies were trapped by fierce Turkish resistance. The death rate mounted, and the Allies eventually withdrew in January 1916.

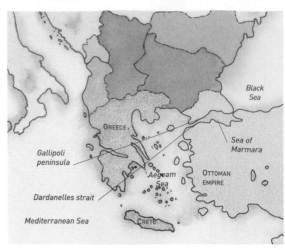

Gallipoli peninsula

The Gallipoli peninsula lies to the north of the Dardanelles. Britain and France wanted direct access from the Mediterranean to the Black Sea and their ally, Russia. But the narrow waterway was controlled by Germany's ally, the Ottoman Empire.

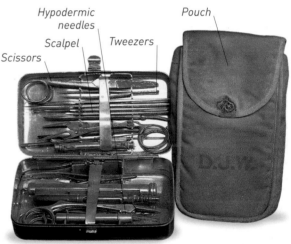

Privately purchased medical kit used by a British officer on the front line

Hypodermic needles — *Pouch* — *Scalpel* — *Tweezers* — *Scissors*

The casualty rate

The treatment and evacuation of casualties from Gallipoli was complicated by the huge numbers of sick soldiers as well as those who were wounded.

Jetty for boats carrying sick and wounded soldiers

The sick beach

On both sides, food was contaminated by flies carrying disease from the many corpses. Dysentery was rife – most of the Anzac troops in a hospital at Anzac Cove (above) had it.

German help

To the Allies' surprise, Gallipoli was strongly defended by Turkish trenches, barbed-wire fences, and artillery. Germany also equipped the Turks with modern pistols, rifles, and machine guns.

Improvised grenades

The fighting at Gallipoli was often at very close range. In a munitions shortage, Allied troops used jam tins to make hand-thrown grenades.

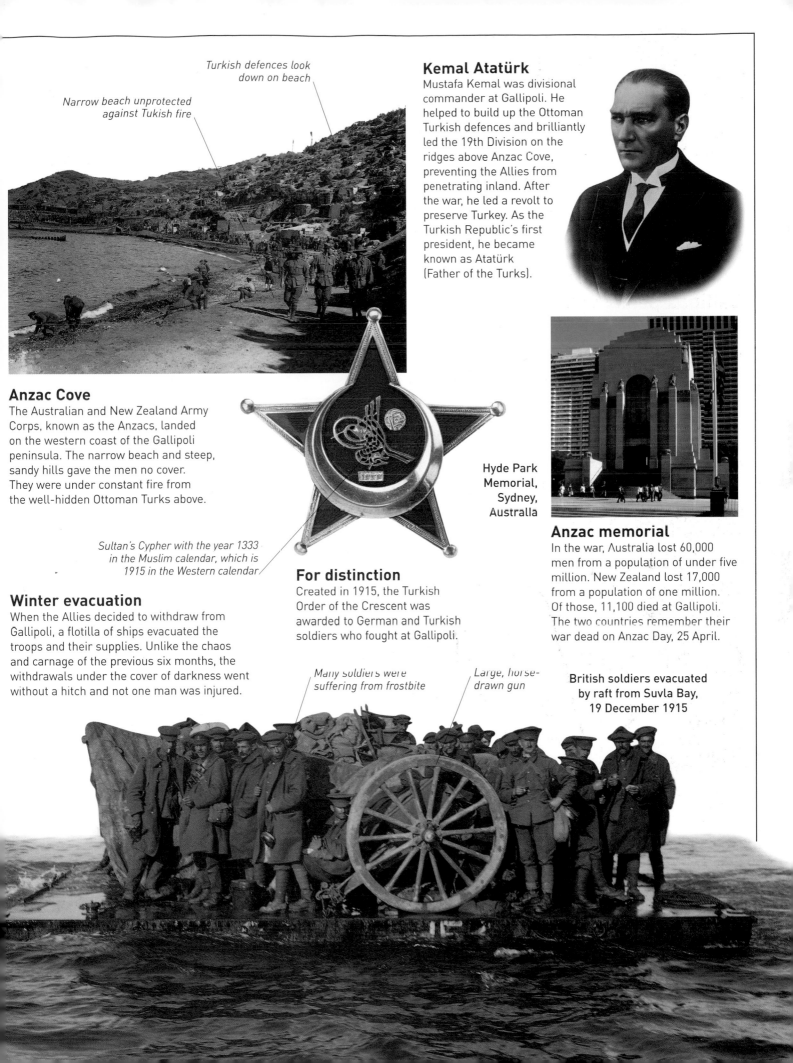

Narrow beach unprotected against Tukish fire

Turkish defences look down on beach

Kemal Atatürk
Mustafa Kemal was divisional commander at Gallipoli. He helped to build up the Ottoman Turkish defences and brilliantly led the 19th Division on the ridges above Anzac Cove, preventing the Allies from penetrating inland. After the war, he led a revolt to preserve Turkey. As the Turkish Republic's first president, he became known as Atatürk (Father of the Turks).

Anzac Cove
The Australian and New Zealand Army Corps, known as the Anzacs, landed on the western coast of the Gallipoli peninsula. The narrow beach and steep, sandy hills gave the men no cover. They were under constant fire from the well-hidden Ottoman Turks above.

Hyde Park Memorial, Sydney, Australla

Sultan's Cypher with the year 1333 in the Muslim calendar, which is 1915 in the Western calendar

For distinction
Created in 1915, the Turkish Order of the Crescent was awarded to German and Turkish soldiers who fought at Gallipoli.

Anzac memorial
In the war, Australia lost 60,000 men from a population of under five million. New Zealand lost 17,000 from a population of one million. Of those, 11,100 died at Gallipoli. The two countries remember their war dead on Anzac Day, 25 April.

Winter evacuation
When the Allies decided to withdraw from Gallipoli, a flotilla of ships evacuated the troops and their supplies. Unlike the chaos and carnage of the previous six months, the withdrawals under the cover of darkness went without a hitch and not one man was injured.

Many soldiers were suffering from frostbite

Large, horse-drawn gun

British soldiers evacuated by raft from Suvla Bay, 19 December 1915

Verdun

On 21 February 1916, Germany launched a massive attack against Verdun, a fortified French city. Close to the German border, Verdun controlled access into eastern France. After a huge, eight-hour artillery bombardment, the German infantry advanced. The French were caught by surprise, but held out. By December, the Germans had been pushed back almost to where they started. The human cost was enormous – more than 400,000 French casualties and 336,831 German casualties.

Burning wreckage
On 25 February, the ancient city of Verdun was evacuated. Many buildings were hit by the artillery bombardment, and even more were destroyed by fires that often raged for days.

General Pétain
General Henri-Philippe Pétain took command of the French forces of Verdun on 25 February. He organized effective defences and army supplies. His rallying cry, "Ils ne passeront pas!" (They shall not pass!), raised French morale.

Exposed concrete fort wall

Machine-gun post

Fort Douaumont
Verdun was protected by three rings of fortifications. Fort Douaumont, in the outer ring, was the strongest of these forts. Defended by just 56 elderly reservists, it fell to the Germans on 25 February.

Background picture: Ruined Verdun cityscape, 1915

Double-breasted greatcoat

Horizon-blue uniform

Haversack

Lebel rifle

Steel helmet

Thick boots with puttees wrapped around the legs

Le poilu
Nicknamed *les poilus,* or "the hairy ones", French infantry bore the brunt of the German attack. Cold, muddy, and wet, they suffered dreadful injuries from shellfire and gas.

At close quarters

Fighting at Verdun was fierce, as both sides repeatedly attacked and counter-attacked the same forts and strategic areas around the city. Advancing attackers were mown down by machine-gun fire from inside the forts. The open ground was too exposed for rescuers to retrieve the dead, and corpses were left to rot. This photograph comes from one of many dramatic films that were made about the war.

> *"What a bloodbath, what horrid images, what a slaughter. I just cannot find the words to express my feelings. Hell cannot be this dreadful."*
>
> *ALBERT JOUBAIRE*
> *FRENCH SOLDIER, VERDUN, 1916*

Surrounding villages

Ornes was one of many villages attacked and captured during the German advance on Verdun. This village, like eight others, was never rebuilt, but is still marked on maps as a sign of remembrance.

Laurel-leaf wreath

Oak-leaf wreath

Head of Marianne, symbol of France

Légion d'Honneur

In tribute to the people of Verdun's suffering, the French president awarded the *Légion d'Honneur* to the city. It is usually given for individual acts of bravery.

The muddy inferno

The land around Verdun is wooded and hilly, with many streams running down to the River Meuse. Heavy rainfall and constant artillery bombardment turned it into a desolate mudbath, where the dead lay half-buried in shell craters and the living had to eat and sleep within centimetres of fallen comrades. This photograph shows the "Ravine de la mort", the Ravine of the Dead.

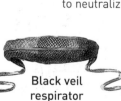

British "Hypo" helmet

Gas attack

On 22 April 1915, French-Algerian troops near the Belgian town of Ypres noticed a greenish-yellow cloud moving towards them from the German front. The cloud was chlorine gas. This was the first time poison gas had been used effectively in war. Many of the troops panicked, for they had no protection against its choking effects. Over the next three years, 1,200,000 soldiers on both sides were gassed, of whom 91,198 died terrible deaths.

Early warning

The first anti-gas masks were crude and often ineffectual. Basic goggles protected the eyes, and mouth pads made of cloth were soaked in chemicals to neutralize the gas.

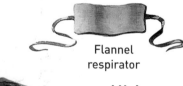

British anti-gas goggles

Black veil respirator

Flannel respirator

Air tube

Chemical filter to neutralize gas

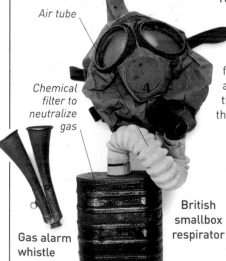

Gas alarm whistle

British smallbox respirator

All-in-one

By the middle of the war, both sides wore protective helmets fitted with face masks, goggles, and respirators. These shielded the eyes, nose, and throat from the potentially lethal effects of gas.

Gassed!

In *Gassed*, a painting from life by the American war artist John Singer Sargent, blinded soldiers are led by sighted colleagues towards a dressing station near Arras in northern France in August 1918.

Phosgene & diphosgene

Diphosgene

Lachrymatory

Diphosgene and sneezing oil

Mustard oil

Gas shells

Gas shells contained liquid gas, which evaporated into the air on impact. Several types of gas were used. Dichlorethylsulphide burned the skin, caused temporary blindness, and, if inhaled, flooded the lungs and led to death from pneumonia.

Glove shrunken by gas

Ordinary glove

Under attack

The first effects of gas were felt on the face and in the eyes, but within seconds it entered the throat. Soldiers coughed and choked as the gas swirled around them. The long-term effects depended on the type of gas used – some soldiers died very quickly, others were blinded for life or suffered awful blisters, or died a lingering death as their lungs collapsed and filled with liquid. This photograph of American troops was used as a demonstration for new recruits.

Hand shrunk

When exposed to some kinds of gas, a leather glove will shrink. This is what happens to a person's lungs when exposed to the same gas.

German gas mask

Eyes not protected

Canvas-covered respirator

Animal welfare

Every living creature was vulnerable to gas, including the many thousands of horses used by both sides to transport men, equipment, and supplies. This German rider and horse both wear gas masks.

In the east

The Western Front was locked in trench warfare, but on the other side of Europe, a much more fluid war took place. The armies of Germany and Austria-Hungary on one side and Russia on the other marched across hundreds of kilometres. The Russians and Austro-Hungarians were badly led and poorly equipped, and suffered huge losses. By 1916, the German army was in full control of the entire Eastern Front.

Tannenberg, 1914
In August 1914, Russia's First and Second armies invaded East Prussia, Germany. The Second Army was surrounded at Tannenberg and forced to surrender on 31 August, with the loss of 150,000 men and all of its artillery (above).

Masurian Lakes, 1914
In September 1914, the Russian First Army had marched to the Masurian Lakes in East Prussia and found itself in danger of being surrounded. German troops dug trenches and other defences (above) and attacked the Russians, who soon withdrew, sustaining more than 100,000 casualties. By the end of September, the Russian threat to Germany was over.

Initial success
During 1914, the Russian army took Austria-Hungary's eastern province of Galicia. In 1915, German troops (above) pushed the Russians back to Russia.

The Italian Front

On 23 May 1915, Italy joined the war on the side of the Allies and prepared to invade its hostile neighbour, Austria-Hungary. Fighting took place on two fronts, to Italy's north and east. The Italian army was ill-prepared and under-equipped for the war, and was unable to break through Austrian defences until its final success at the Battle of Vittorio-Veneto in October 1918.

The Isonzo River

The Isonzo flowed between the mountains of Austria-Hungary and the plains of northeast Italy. After 11 battles along the river, victory fell to the Austrians, with German support, at Caporetto in 1917.

Unwilling to fight

By the end of 1916, many Russian soldiers were refusing to fight. Starving and badly treated, they saw litte reason to risk their lives in a war they did not believe in. Such low morale led, in part, to the Russian Revoution of 1917.

Russian troops marching to defend the newly captured city of Przemysl in Austrian Galicia

Italian alpinists

Most of the 640-km (400-mile) Italian frontier with Austria-Hungary lay in the Italian Alps. Both sides used trained alpine troops to fight in mountainous terrain.

War in the desert

World War I was not restricted to Europe. A major conflict took place in the Middle East, which was largely controlled by the Turkish Ottoman Empire. British and Indian troops invaded Mesopotamia (now Iraq) in 1914 and took Baghdad in 1917. A large British force, under General Allenby, captured Palestine and the Syrian capital of Damascus. In Arabia, Bedouin soldiers under the guidance of T.E. Lawrence rose in revolt against Turkish rule.

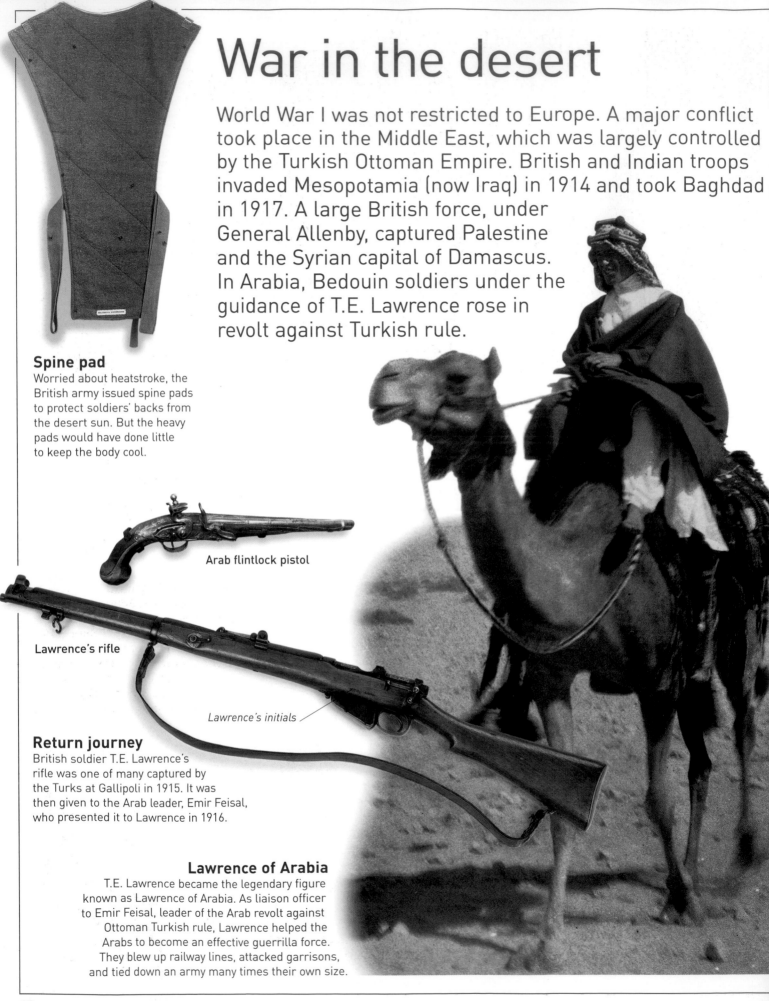

Spine pad
Worried about heatstroke, the British army issued spine pads to protect soldiers' backs from the desert sun. But the heavy pads would have done little to keep the body cool.

Arab flintlock pistol

Lawrence's rifle

Lawrence's initials

Return journey
British soldier T.E. Lawrence's rifle was one of many captured by the Turks at Gallipoli in 1915. It was then given to the Arab leader, Emir Feisal, who presented it to Lawrence in 1916.

Lawrence of Arabia
T.E. Lawrence became the legendary figure known as Lawrence of Arabia. As liaison officer to Emir Feisal, leader of the Arab revolt against Ottoman Turkish rule, Lawrence helped the Arabs to become an effective guerrilla force. They blew up railway lines, attacked garrisons, and tied down an army many times their own size.

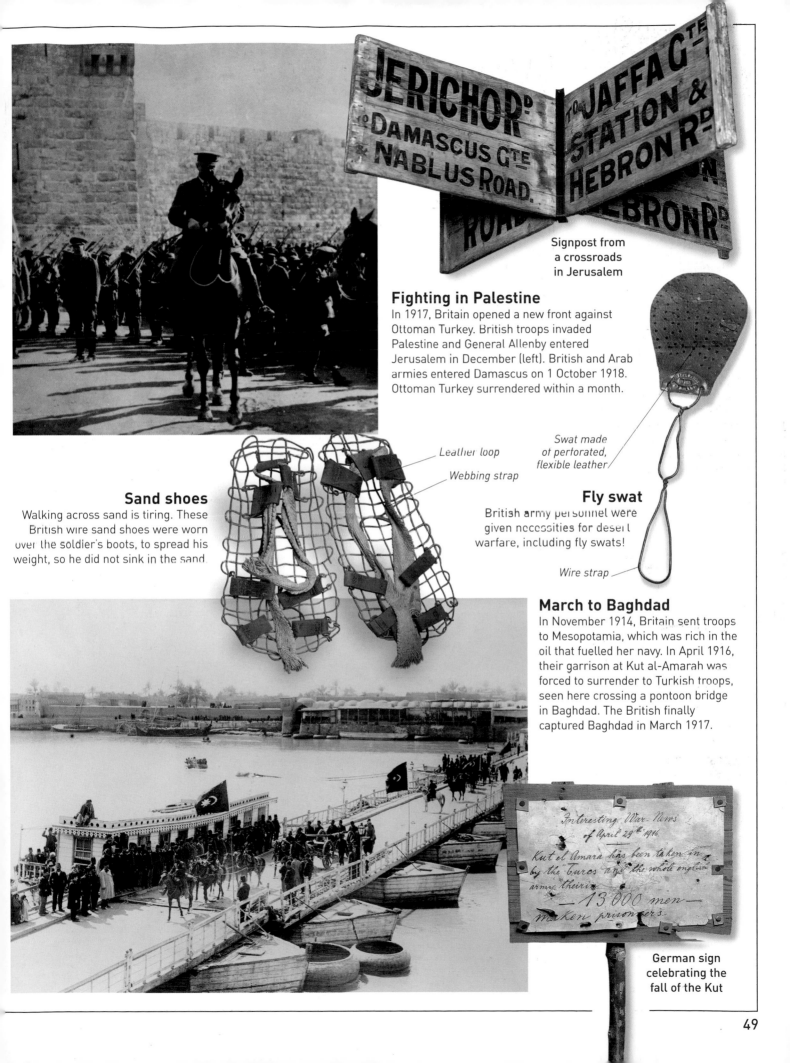

Signpost from
a crossroads
in Jerusalem

Fighting in Palestine

In 1917, Britain opened a new front against
Ottoman Turkey. British troops invaded
Palestine and General Allenby entered
Jerusalem in December (left). British and Arab
armies entered Damascus on 1 October 1918.
Ottoman Turkey surrendered within a month.

Leather loop

Webbing strap

Swat made
of perforated,
flexible leather

Sand shoes

Walking across sand is tiring. These
British wire sand shoes were worn
over the soldier's boots, to spread his
weight, so he did not sink in the sand.

Fly swat

British army personnel were
given necessities for desert
warfare, including fly swats!

Wire strap

March to Baghdad

In November 1914, Britain sent troops
to Mesopotamia, which was rich in the
oil that fuelled her navy. In April 1916,
their garrison at Kut al-Amarah was
forced to surrender to Turkish troops,
seen here crossing a pontoon bridge
in Baghdad. The British finally
captured Baghdad in March 1917.

Interesting War News
of April 29th 1916
Kut el Amara has been taken in
by the Turcs and the whole english
army their
— 13,000 men —
taken prisoners.

German sign
celebrating the
fall of the Kut

49

Espionage

Both sides suspected the other of employing hundreds of spies in enemy territory, but most espionage work consisted of eavesdropping on enemy communications. Code-breaking or cryptography was crucial, as both sides sent and received coded messages by radio and telegraph. Cryptographers devised complex codes to ensure the safe transit of their own messages while using their skills to intercept and break coded enemy messages.

Lightweight, but strong, string attaches parachute to bird

Corselet made of linen and padded to protect bird

Pigeon post
Over 500,000 pigeons were used to carry messages between intelligence agents and their home bases. The pigeons were dropped by parachute into occupied areas and collected by agents. Messages were attached to their legs, and they were released to fly back to their lofts.

Edith Cavell
British-born Edith Cavell ran a nursing school in the Belgian city of Brussels (above). When the Germans occupied the city in August 1914, she took in up to 200 British soldiers trapped behind enemy lines. When the Germans had her shot as a spy in October 1915, her story provided powerful propaganda for the Allies.

In miniature
Pigeons can't carry much weight. This message is written on the small "pigeon post" form used by the German army. Long messages were photographed with a camera that reduced them to the size of a microdot – 300 times smaller than the original.

Secret ink
Special ink was used to write invisible messages on paper. The message could be read later when treated with a chemical to make the words visible.

German invisible ink

Invisible ink bottle

Front of button

Coded message on back of button

Button message
Tiny and unobtrusive, coded messages were stamped on to the back of buttons sewn on to coats or jackets.

Pocket camera

This miniature camera disguised as a fob watch was used to take secret photographs in German East Africa (now Tanzania).

Lens cap

Camera lens

Shutter release

Reading the enemy

Army intelligence officers, such as this British soldier, played a vital role in examining and understanding captured enemy documents. They pieced together information about enemy plans or morale, and sent it to the military high command.

Hidden messages

Two Dutch agents sent to England to spy for Germany pretended to be cigar importers. They used their cigar orders as codes for the ships they observed in Portsmouth Harbour. In 1915, they were caught and executed.

Cigars slit open in search of hidden messages

Aid to escape

This food tin was sent to British Lieutenant Jack Shaw at a German prisoner-of-war camp in 1918. It contained maps, wire cutters, and compasses for a mass escape.

Rolled-up map of France

Lead weights to make the tin the correct weight

Compass

Mata Hari

Dutch-born Margaretha Zelle was a famous dancer who used the stage name Mata Hari. She had many high-ranking lovers, who revealed confidential information, which she passed to the French secret service. When fed false information by a German diplomat, she was shot as a German spy in 1917.

Tank warfare

In November 1917, at the Battle of Cambrai, the British-invented tank first displayed its full potential. An artillery bombardment would have made the ground impossible for the infantry to cross. Instead, tanks flattened barbed-wire, crossed enemy trenches, and shielded the advancing infantry. Tanks played a vital role in the Allied advances throughout 1918.

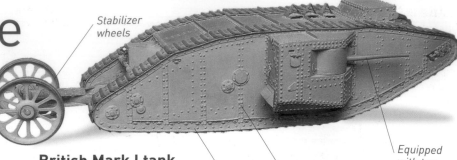

Stabilizer wheels

British Mark I tank
The first tank to see action was the British Mark 1 tank. Of the 49 built for the Battle of the Somme on 15 September 1916, only 18 were judged fit for battle.

Carried crew of eight men

Total weight of 28,450 kg (62,722 lb)

Equipped with two six-pounder guns and four machine guns

Toughened leather skull cap

Protect and survive
British tank crews wore leather helmets with visors and chainmail mouthpieces to protect their heads against specks of hot metal that flew off the inside of the hull when the tank was hit by bullets.

Leather visor

Chainmail mouthpiece

German A7V tank

A7V tank
In 1918, too late to make any real impact, the Germans built the huge A7V, a 33,500-kg (73,855-lb) machine with six machine guns and a crew of 18. Only 20 A7Vs were constructed.

British Mark V tank

Inside a tank

The tank was hot, fume-ridden, and badly ventilated, making the crew sick or even faint. The heat was sometimes so great in light tanks that it exploded the ammunition.

Rear entry hatch

Driver's entry hatch

Lid for driver's entry hatch

Driver's visor

ME9828

T 9171

Iron caterpillar track

The driver and gunner were squashed in the front of the tank

Six men sat around the engine manning the guns

Six cylinder engine

Machine-gun port

British Mark V tank

The British Mark V tank first saw action in July 1918. It had two six-pounder guns and four machine guns, and had a crew of eight.

Driving a tank

Early tanks were driven by two people, each controlling one track, and had a range of just 40 km (25 miles). Later tanks had a single driver, but they were still vulnerable to enemy shellfire, and often broke down, as here during the British assault on Arras in 1917.

Crossing the trenches

For wide trenches, British tanks were fitted with circular metal bundles that dropped into the trench to form a bridge. This line of Mark V tanks is moving in to attack German trenches in autumn 1918.

The USA joins in

When war broke out in Europe in 1914, the USA remained neutral. In 1917, Germany decided to attack all foreign shipping to try to limit supplies to Britain. It also tried to divert US attention from Europe by encouraging its neighbour, Mexico, to invade. This action outraged the US government, and as more US ships were sunk, President Wilson declared war on Germany. This was now a world war.

Uncle Sam
The all-American figure of Uncle Sam was based on Kitchener's pose for British recruiting posters (see p. 14). Beneath his pointing finger were the words "I WANT YOU FOR THE US ARMY".

British medal suggesting the attack on SS *Lusitania* was planned

SS *Lusitania*
On 7 May 1915, the passenger ship SS *Lusitania* was sunk off the Irish coast by German torpedoes, for allegedly carrying munitions. The victims included 128 US citizens. Their death did much to turn the US public against Germany and towards the Allies.

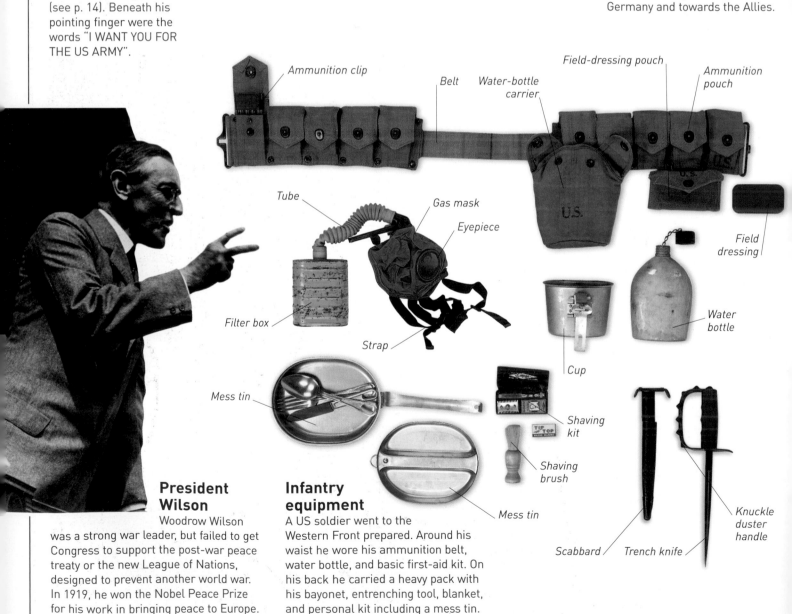

President Wilson
Woodrow Wilson was a strong war leader, but failed to get Congress to support the post-war peace treaty or the new League of Nations, designed to prevent another world war. In 1919, he won the Nobel Peace Prize for his work in bringing peace to Europe.

Infantry equipment
A US soldier went to the Western Front prepared. Around his waist he wore his ammunition belt, water bottle, and basic first-aid kit. On his back he carried a heavy pack with his bayonet, entrenching tool, blanket, and personal kit including a mess tin.

Labels: Ammunition clip · Belt · Water-bottle carrier · Field-dressing pouch · Ammunition pouch · Tube · Gas mask · Eyepiece · Field dressing · Filter box · Strap · Cup · Water bottle · Mess tin · Shaving kit · Shaving brush · Mess tin · Scabbard · Trench knife · Knuckle duster handle

Gun fire

The US First Army first saw major action in September 1918 at St Mihiel, south of Verdun, France, in an Allied attack on German lines. Here an artillery crew fires a field gun, surrounded by shell cases.

For heroism

Introduced in 1918, the Distinguished Service Cross was awarded for extreme heroism against an armed enemy.

Securing strap for pack contents

M1905 Springfield bayonet

Haversack

Entrenching tool

Blanket or greatcoat roll

Assembled kit, US infantry equipment

Keeping in touch

Many US soldiers had hardly left their town or state before, let alone gone abroad. Stationed in France, where they could not speak the language, many were homesick. They wrote often to family and friends, and waited for letters, postcards, and food parcels in return.

Mines and mud

Air tubes

To the rescue
Fumes from a gas attack or a shell burst near a tunnel entrance could suffocate the men inside. This German breathing apparatus was for rescue parties.

For much of the war on the Western Front, the two sides faced each other in rows of heavily fortified trenches. Both excavated tunnels and mines deep under enemy lines and packed them with explosives, ready to be detonated when an attack began. Counter-mines were dug to destroy enemy mines before they could be finished. Vast mines were exploded by the British at the Battle of the Somme on 1 July 1916, but their most effective use was at the start of the Battle of Passchendaele.

— Headpiece

— Straps to hold mouthpiece in place

— Nose clip

— Air tube

— Breathing bag was carried on chest

— Air from oxygen cylinders carried on the back entered the breathing bag through this valve

"Prote"

Oxygen relief
This British breathing apparatus, like the German equipment on the left, fed compressed oxygen to a mouthpiece to help a miner breathe.

Background picture: a British mine explodes under German lines at the Battle of the Somme, 1 July 1916

Sappers at work
British artist David Bomberg painted members of the Royal Engineers, known as sappers, digging and reinforcing this underground trench.

> *"It is horrible. You often wish you were dead, there is no shelter, we are lying in water... our clothes do not dry."*
>
> *GERMAN SOLDIER, PASSCHENDAELE, 1917*

Waterlogged
The water table around Ypres was very high, so the trenches were built above ground by banking up earth and sandbags. Even so, the trenches were constantly flooded. Pumping out mines and trenches, as these Australian tunnellers are doing at Hooge, Belgium, in September 1917, was an essential, never-ending task.

Passchendaele

In 1917, the British planned to attack the German front line around Ypres, Belgium, and then seize the channel ports used by German submarines as a base to attack British shipping. The Battle of Messines began on 7 June 1917. After a huge artillery bombardment, 19 mines packed with one million tonnes (1.1 million US tons) of explosives blew up under the German lines on Messines Ridge. The noise could be heard in London 220 km (140 miles) away. The village and ridge of Passchendaele were captured on 10 November 1917, then lost again. In summer 1918, the Allies re-captured and kept the ground.

Muddy quagmire
Heavy rainfall and constant shelling at Passchendaele created a deadly mudbath. Many injured men died as they were unable to lift themselves clear of the cloying mud. Stretcher bearers were barely able to carry the wounded to dressing stations.

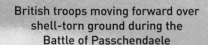

British troops moving forward over shell-torn ground during the Battle of Passchendaele

The final year

In early 1918, the war looked to be turning in favour of Germany. Russia had withdrawn from the war, so Germany could now focus on the Western Front, and most US troops had yet to reach France. But the Allied blockade of her ports kept Germany short of vital supplies, food was scarce, and strikes and mutinies were rife. Ottoman Turkey, Bulgaria, and Austria-Hungary collapsed under Allied attack. By early November, Germany stood alone. On 7 November, a German delegation crossed the front line to discuss peace terms with the Allies.

New leader
In 1917, Vladimir Lenin, the anti-war leader of the Bolshevik (Communist) Party, became the new ruler of Russia.

Germans and Russians celebrate the cease-fire on the Eastern Front, 1917

Russia pulls out

The Russian government became increasingly unpopular as the war progressed. In February 1917, a revolution overthrew the Tsar, but the new government continued the war. A second revolution in October brought the Bolshevik Party to power. A ceasefire was agreed with Germany, and in March 1918 Russia signed the Treaty of Brest-Litovsk and withdrew from the war.

The Ludendorff Offensive
General Ludendorff launched a huge attack on the Western Front on 21 March 1918, hoping to defeat Britain and France before US troops arrived. Germany advanced almost 64 km (40 miles) by July, but suffered 500,000 casualties.

French and British troops in action during the Ludendorff Offensive

3 March Treaty of Brest-Litovsk; Russia leaves the war
21 March Vast Ludendorff Offensive on the Western Front

15 July Last German offensive launched on Western Front
18 July French counter-attack begins on the Marne

8 August British launch offensive near Amiens
12 September Americans launch offensive at St Mihiel

14 September Allies attack Bulgaria from Greece
25 September Bulgaria seeks peace

Battle of the Marne

On 18 July 1918, French and US forces counter-attacked against the German advance on the River Marne, east of Paris, and began to push the Germans eastwards. By 6 August, the Germans had lost 168,000 men, many buried where they fell on the battlefields (left). The Allies now had the upper hand.

French soldiers identifying German dead before burial

Crossing the line

On 8 August 1918, a huge British offensive began near Amiens. Allied troops were pushing towards the heavily fortified Hindenburg Line, the Germans' fall-back defensive position. On 29 September, the British 46th North Midland Division took the bridge at Riqueval. They had broken the Line at last, and posed for this photograph.

Many French children did not remember life before the German occupation of their towns and cities

Background picture: German troops advancing at the Somme, April 1918

French children march alongside the Allied army

The last days

By 5 October, the Allies had breached the entire Hindenburg Line. Both sides suffered great casualties as the German army was pushed steadily eastwards. As the British and French recaptured towns and cities lost in 1914, including Lille (left), the German retreat was turning into a defeat.

27 September British begin to breach Hindenburg Line
1 October British take Ottoman Turkish-held Damascus

6 October German government starts to negotiate an armistice
24 October Italy attacks Austria-Hungary at Vittorio-Veneto

29 October German fleet mutinies
30 October Ottoman Turkey agrees an armistice
4 November Austria-Hungary

agrees an armistice
9 November The Kaiser abdicates
11 November Armistice between Germany and the Allies; war ends

Armistice and peace

At 11 am on the 11th day of the 11th month of 1918, the guns of Europe fell silent after more than four years of war. The Allies wanted to make sure that Germany would never go to war again. The eventual peace treaty redrew the map of Europe and forced Germany to pay huge damages to the Allies. German armed forces were reduced and Germany lost a great deal of land and all of her overseas colonies.

Carriage talks

On 7 November 1918, a German delegation met the Allied commander-in-chief, Marshal Foch, in his railway carriage in the forest of Compiègne. On 11 November, they signed an armistice agreement.

Displaced people

Many refugees, like these Lithuanians, were displaced during the war. The end of hostilities allowed thousands of refugees to return to their newly liberated countries. There were also as many as 6.5 million prisoners of war who had to be repatriated. This complex task was finally achieved by autumn 1919.

Spreading the news

News of the armistice spread around the world in minutes, in newspapers and telegrams, and by word of mouth in every neighbourhood.

Vive la paix!

In Paris (below), Allied soldiers joined locals in an inpromptu procession. In London, women and children danced in the streets while their men prepared to leave the front. In Germany, there was shock and relief that the fighting was over.

Signing the treaty

These soldiers watching the signing of the Treaty of Versailles had waited a long time for this moment. The Allies first met their German counterparts in January 1919. Negotiations almost broke down several times before a final agreement was reached in June 1919.

The Treaty of Versailles

The peace treaty that ended the war was signed in the Hall of Mirrors in the Palace of Versailles near Paris, on 28 June 1919. William Orpen's painting shows the four Allied leaders watching the German delegates sign the treaty.

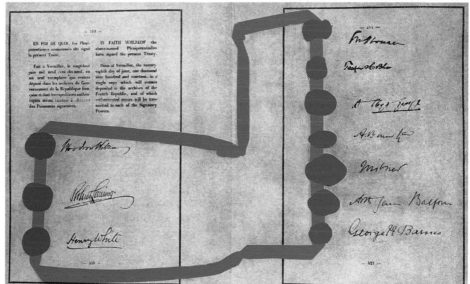

The peace treaties

The Treaty of Versailles was signed by representatives of the Allied powers and Germany. Over the next year, in the Allies' treaties with Austria, Bulgaria, Turkey, and Hungary, a new map of Europe emerged.

The Treaty of Versailles

General Foch

Georges Clemenceau

David Lloyd George

Vittorio Orlando

Giorgio Sonnino

The victorious allies

The negotiations in Paris were dominated by the Big Four: French premier Georges Clemenceau (supported by General Foch), British premier David Lloyd George, Italian premier Vittorio Orlando (seen here with his foreign minister, Giorgio Sonnino), and the US president Woodrow Wilson.

The cost of war

The human cost of this war was huge. Over 65 million men fought, of whom more than half were killed or injured – eight million killed, two million died of illness and disease, 21.2 million wounded, and 7.8 million taken prisoner or missing. About 6.6 million civilians also perished. Among the combatant nations, apart from the USA, there was barely a family that had not lost at least one son or brother. European economies were ruined, while the USA emerged as a major world power.

One life
A soldier remembers a fallen comrade during the Battle of Passchendaele in 1917, but many men were engulfed in mud, their graves unmarked.

The unknown soldier
Many of the dead were too badly disfigured to be identified. Thousands more just disappeared, presumed dead. Tombs of an unknown warrior stand at the Arc de Triomphe, Paris, and Westminster Abbey, London.

Aftercare
For thousands of disfigured and disabled soldiers, reconstructive surgery helped repair facial damage, masks and prosthetics covered horrible disfigurements, and artificial limbs gave some mobility.

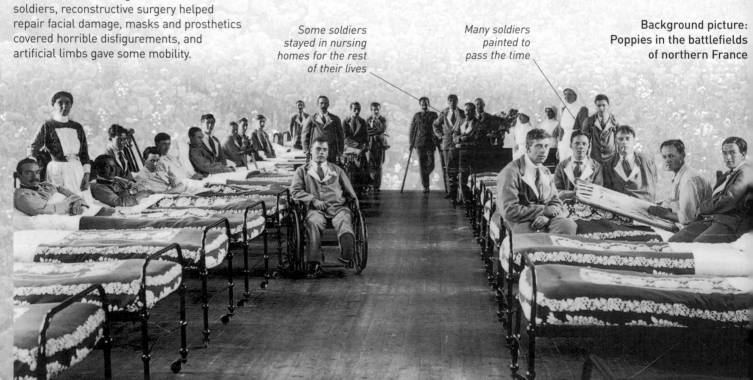

Some soldiers stayed in nursing homes for the rest of their lives

Many soldiers painted to pass the time

Background picture:
Poppies in the battlefields of northern France

War memorials

The Western Front is lined with graveyards and memorials to the fallen, including 130,000 unknown French and German soldiers at Douaumont, Verdun (below).

Prussian Iron Cross

Victoria Cross (V.C.)

Mementos

Soldiers on both sides of the Western Front pressed wild flowers as mementos. Private Jack Mudd sent this red Flanders poppy to his wife Lizzie before he was killed at Passchendaele. The poppies feature in the wartime poem *In Flanders Fields*, and inspired the British Legion to sell paper poppies to raise money for injured soldiers and as a sign of remembrance for the dead.

For gallantry

Every combatant nation awarded medals for bravery to its soldiers, civilians, and allies – including five million Iron Crosses in Germany, over two million Croix de Guerre in France, and 576 Victoria Crosses across the British Empire.

French *Croix de Guerre*

Did you know?

BITE-SIZED FACTS

✠ In 1917, explosives blowing up beneath the German lines on Messines Ridge at Ypres in Belgium could be heard in London, 220 km (140 miles) away.

✠ Every British soldier was given his boots in time to wear them in and, from the Somme onwards, his own steel helmet. Specialist equipment was kept in communal stores – handed on from unit to unit.

Left to right, British Army specialist clothing for transport drivers, flame thrower operators, trench raiding (in winter camouflage), and airmen

✠ Flame throwers were first used by the Germans. They fired jets of flame as far as 40 m (131 ft).

✠ Russia had the largest army. It mobilized 12 million troops during the course of the war. More than three-quarters were killed, wounded, or went missing in action.

✠ Built in 1915, the first prototype tank, "Little Willie", carried a crew of three and had a top speed of 4.8 kph (3 mph). At first, Brititsh tanks were split into "males" and "females". Male tanks had cannons, while female tanks had heavy machine guns.

✠ Tunnellers laid mines on the Western Front. Sometimes underground fights broke out, if they dug into an enemy tunnel by mistake.

✠ Prague-born Walter Trier (1890–1951) produced political cartoons. The famous work above shows Europe in 1914 on the eve of World War I, with the national leaders threatening one another.

Map of Europe in 1914, drawn by cartoonist Walter Trier

✠ Food was prepared in field kitchens that could be several kilometres behind the front line. It was impossible to take transport vehicles into the trench, so food had to be carried to the front on foot.

✠ The Pool of Peace is a 12-m (40-ft) deep lake near Messines, Belgium. It fills a crater made in 1917 when the British detonated a mine containing 40 tonnes (44 US tons) of explosives (see p. 57)

Filling a Thermos container that kept food hot

A German messenger dog laying telegraph wire

✠ To help military communications, messenger dogs carried orders to the front line in capsules strapped to their bodies, while other dogs were trained to lay down telegraph wire!

QUESTIONS AND ANSWERS

Modern-day camouflage

Q Who was "Big Bertha"?

A Weighing 43,700 kg (96,342 lb), "Big Bertha" was a howitzer used by the Germans in World War I. Its designer, Gustav Krupp, named the weapon after his wife. It took its crew of 200 men six hours or more to assemble. It could be transported to its firing position by tractor and could fire a 930-kg (2,050-lb) shell a distance of 15 km (9.3 miles). Big Bertha's first successes were at Liege in Belgium. The 12 forts ringing the city were destroyed in three days.

Q Why did soldiers keep animals?

A Most animals that travelled with the army had a job to do. Mules, horses,

Soldiers with their rabbits and chickens

and camels transported heavy supplies. Messenger dogs and pigeons carried important communications. Away from the front line, some soldiers kept animals for food – rabbits for the cooking pot or hens for their eggs.

Q How did soldiers camouflage themselves?

A For the first time in a major conflict, soldiers made use of camouflage. They wore khaki uniforms that blended in with the background. Steel helmets were often painted with matt paint mixed with sand or sawdust so that they would not reflect the light; other times they were smeared with mud or covered with sacking from sandbags. Soldiers also used sacking or netting to hide their equipment from the reconnaissance aircraft patrolling the skies.

Q How did soldiers know when to put on their gas masks?

A There were soldiers on lookout duty night and day. These sentries used whatever they could find to raise the alarm – bells, rattles, whistles, or their own voice. When the soldiers heard the alarm, they put on their gas masks as quickly as they could – hopefully before the deadly gas drifted into the trench.

Metal bell sounds the alarm

A sentry on duty

Q Why were tanks called tanks?

A While it was being developed, the tank was known as a "landship". However, there were fears that this name was too obvious, spies might wonder why so many of these objects were being produced, and the Germans might catch on to the new invention. The British had to come up with a believable name. They decided that, with its rectangular body shape, perhaps it could be passed off as a water storage tank, and called it a "tank" instead.

Sentry wears mask to protect from gas attack

People and places

So many people played an important role in planning or fighting World War I, but here are some of the key names and battle sites.

General Joseph Joffre

King George V of Britain

General Ferdinand Foch

President Raymond Poincaré of France

General Sir Douglas Haig

IMPORTANT PERSONALITIES

Alexei Brusilov (1853–1926)
General Brusilov broke Austro-Hungarian lines in 1916 and took command of Russian forces on the Eastern Front in 1917.

Luigi Cadorna (1850–1928)
The general in charge of the Italian army had only one success – the recapture of Gorizia in 1916.

Russian General Brusilov

Ferdinand Foch (1851–1929)
Artillery specialist Ferdinand Foch successfully led the French at the Marne. By 1918, he was co-ordinating all the Allied forces on the Western Front.

Anthony Fokker (1890–1939)
Dutch designer Anthony Fokker developed the first fighter plane with a forward-facing synchronized machine gun. Germany used 40 different Fokker aircrafts during the war.

René Fonck (1894–1953)
Frenchman René Fonck was the Allies' most successful fighter pilot. He shot down 75 planes.

Douglas Haig (1861–1928)
Britain's top general on the Western Front was Sir Douglas Haig. He ordered the offensives at the Somme and Passchendaele, as well as the final, successful Allied offensive.

Paul von Hindenburg (1847–1934)
Early in the war, Paul von Hindenburg successfully led the Germans against the Russians. By 1916, he commanded all German land forces. His Hindenburg Line withstood attack from 1917 to 1918.

Joseph Joffre (1852–1931)
Joseph Joffre was Commander of the French army. After heavy losses on the Western Front, he was replaced in 1916.

T.E. Lawrence (1888–1935)
"Lawrence of Arabia" led an Arab revolt against the Turks in the Middle East, which he described in his book, *The Seven Pillars of Wisdom*.

Rittmeister von Richthofen (1892–1918)
Germany's "Red Baron" shot down 80 planes – more than any other World War I pilot. He was shot down near Amiens.

Maximilian von Spee (1861–1914)
This German admiral sank two British cruisers off Chile. His own ship, the *Scharnhorst*, sank near the Falklands.

Gabriel Voisin (1880–1973)
French-born designer Gabriel Voisin is famous for his Voisin III (the first Allied plane to shoot down an enemy) and his Voisin V bomber, armed with a cannon.

Margaretha Zelle (1876–1917)
Dutch-born "Mata Hari" denied being a double agent, but may have spied for both the French and Germans. The French executed her in 1917.

Propeller rotation was synchronized with gunfire

Anthony Fokker with his Fokker DL aircraft

Aircraft designer Gabriel Voisin (right)

MAJOR BATTLES

Tanks during the Amiens offensive

Amiens
In August 1918, General Rawlinson led a successful Allied offensive to retake the Amiens Line. On the first day, the Allies advanced 12 km (7.5 miles).

Cambrai
General Haig took the Germans by surprise in November 1917 when he attacked them at Cambrai, France. At first, the Allies gained ground, but the Germans soon regained their position. The estimated casualties were 45,000 British soldiers and 50,000 Germans.

Gaza
In March 1917, General Dobell led a British attack on Turkish-held Gaza, a key port on the way to Palestine. Gaza finally fell in November, after bombardment from ships offshore.

A British dressing station at Cambrai

Heligoland Bight
In August 1914, British ships attacked German vessels near the naval base on Heligoland in the North Sea. In the ensuing battle, the British sank three cruisers and a destroyer.

Jutland
May 1916 saw the war's only major sea battle, off the Danish coast of Jutland. Both sides claimed victory. The British suffered the heaviest losses, but had maintained control of the North Sea.

The Retreat from Mons (1927) by Lady Elizabeth Butler

Mons
The British Expeditionary Force met the advancing German army at Mons, France, in August 1914. The Germans suffered heavy losses but forced the British back to the River Marne.

Passchendaele
The Battle of Passchendaele, Belgium, began in July 1917. First, the Allies spent ten days bombarding the Germans. Their advance slowed by torrential rain, they finally took the ridge in November.

Somme
The Battle of the Somme, France, lasted from July to November 1916. The Allies suffered 620,000 casualties (including 58,000 on the first day) and the Germans an estimated 500,000 casualties.

Verdun
The Germans attacked the garrison town of Verdun, France, in February 1916. They outnumbered the French five to one at first, but the battle ran on for 10 months and nearly a million died.

Vittorio-Veneto
In one of the last offensives of the war, the Italians retook Vittorio-Veneto on 29 October 1918. The Austro-Hungarians had retreated the day before.

Ypres
The Belgian town of Ypres was taken by the Germans in August 1914, but the British recaptured it in October. A second battle of Ypres took place in April and May 1915 and a third, Passchendaele, in 1917.

A British field kitchen at the Somme, 1916

Find out more

There are many ways you can find out more about World War I. Ask older generations of your family if they remember stories about relatives who fought in the war. You can find lots more information online and at your library. War museums, television documentaries, and old war films also bring the war to life.

Poppy symbolizes remembrance

Remembrance day
Each year, on the Sunday nearest to 11 November, services are held at local and national war memorials to commemorate the fallen.

The Tank Museum
The world's largest tank museum at Bovington, Dorset, is home to the first tank prototype, Little Willie, and runs lots of special events.

Arc de Triomphe
Built by Napoleon, the Arc de Triomphe in Paris, France, now keeps alive the memory of the millions of soldiers killed in World War I, marked by a flame of remembrance and the tomb of an unknown soldier.

French tricolour (national flag) is flown each year on 11 November

Anzac veteran wears wartime medals and decorations

Anzac Day
In Australia and New Zealand, 25 April is Anzac Day. Parades and ceremonies mark the lives of the thousands of Anzac soldiers who died at Gallipoli, Turkey, in 1915.

War films

A great many movies have been made about World War I. Not all are based on solid fact, but they give a flavour of the time. One of the best is *Lawrence of Arabia* (1962). Directed by David Lean, it starred Peter O'Toole (above) in the title role.

USEFUL WEBSITES

- Information about the centenary commemorations that marks the beginning of World War I: **www.iwm.org.uk/centenary**
- First-person accounts, sound files, movies, and animations, plus a curriculum-related kids' area: **http://www.bbc.co.uk/ww1**
- A multimedia site about World War I: **www.firstworldwar.com**

PLACES TO VISIT

AUSTRALIAN WAR MEMORIAL, CANBERRA, AUSTRALIA

- Gallipoli gallery with life-size reconstructions and diorama.
- Western Front exhibition depicting trench warfare, including video footage.
- "Lone Pine Tree" grown from a seed sent from Gallipoli by a soldier to his mother.

HISTORIAL DE LA GRANDE GUERRE, PERONNE, FRANCE

- Thousands of wartime artefacts, with themes including children and prisoners.
- Offers "Circuit of Remembrance" – a tour of key battle sites in northern France.

IMPERIAL WAR MUSEUM, LONDON, UK

- World War I tank, plus a dedicated gallery with firearms, uniforms, posters, medals, and other artefacts.
- Walk-through "Trench Experience" with sights, sounds, and smells that bring the Battle of the Somme to life.
- Exhibits on the developments of aircraft and pilot "aces".

THE ROYAL SIGNALS MUSEUM, BLANDFORD, UK

- Special area devoted to new technologies in World War I, including the development of the military telephone and wireless.
- Exhibits on the use of animals in war.

Life-size model shows army doctor dressing wounds

Imperial War Museum, London

The Trench Experience at the Imperial War Museum uses lights, sounds, and smells to help visitors feel how terrifying trench life was.

Sculpture shows parents mourning the loss of their son

War monument

Many artists and writers have shared their feelings about World War I in their work. Kathe Kollwitz (1867–1945) made this statue for the German war cemetery at Roggevelde, Belgium. Her son, Peter, is buried there.

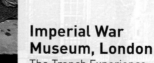

Glossary

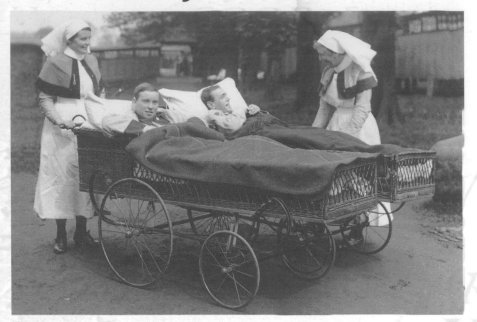

Nurses wheel convalescent soldiers around the hospital grounds

ABDICATE Give up office or power.

ALLIANCE A group of allies, who have agreed to act in co-operation.

ALTITUDE Height above sea level.

AMMUNITION Bullets and shells fired from weapons.

AMPUTATION Surgical removal of a body part, such as an arm or leg.

ANZAC Member of the Australian and New Zealand Army Corps.

ARMISTICE End of hostilities. Armistice Day, now known as Remembrance Sunday, is commemorated each year on the Sunday closest to 11 November.

ARMS RACE Rivalry between nations to build up weaponry, or armaments.

ARTILLERY Heavy weapons, such as cannons, and the sections of the armed forces that use them.

ASSASSINATION The murder of someone for political purposes.

BATTERY The place where a cannon, or other form of artillery, is positioned.

BAYONET A blade fixed to a rifle or other firearm, to stab the enemy when fighting at close quarters.

BULLY BEEF A name for corned beef.

BUNKER An underground bomb shelter.

CAMOUFLAGE Colouring designed to blend in with the background. In World War I, this was mostly used to hide gun positions, although some soldiers blackened their faces before night patrols and snipers wore camouflaged suits.

CAVALRY Originally, soldiers on horseback, but also soldiers using tanks and other motorized forms of transport.

CLIP A device for carrying and rapidly loading rifle ammunition.

COLONY A dependency, or place, which is ruled by a foreign nation.

CONSCIENTIOUS OBJECTOR Someone who refuses to fight for moral reasons.

CONSCRIPT Someone who is forced by law to fight in the army.

Small box respirator gas mask

CONVALESCENT Someone who has been seriously injured or ill and is slowly recovering.

CONVOY Merchant ships travelling together, protected by a naval escort.

CRYPTOGRAPHY The study and creation of secret codes.

DETONATE To explode or cause to explode.

DYSENTERY An infection of the intestines that causes diarrhoea and bloody faeces and was responsible for many casualties.

EMPLACEMENT A mound or platform from which guns are fired.

ENLIST Call or sign up to the armed forces.

ENTENTE A friendly agreement or informal alliance between nations.

An intelligence officer inspects aerial photographs of enemy trenches

EVACUATION Moving people away from a place where they are in danger.

FLOTILLA A fleet or group of small ships.

FRONT LINE The border between enemy territories, where the fighting is.

FUSELAGE The body of an aeroplane.

GAS In the context of war, a poisonous gas, such as chlorine, used as a weapon to choke, blind, or kill the enemy.

GRENADE A small bomb hurled by hand.

GUERRILLA A fighter in a unit dedicated to sabotage and hit-and-run attacks. From the Spanish for "small war".

TOGETHER WE WIN

UNITED STATES SHIPPING BOARD ——— EMERGENCY FLEET CORPORATION

An American propaganda poster

HOWITZER A short gun that fired high.

INCENDIARY Describes a bomb, bullet, or other device designed to cause fire.

INFANTRY Foot soldiers.

INTELLIGENCE Useful military or political information, or the spies who gather it.

KNOT A unit for measuring a ship's speed. One knot equals 1.85 kph (1.15 mph).

MACHINE GUN An automatic gun that fires bullets in rapid succession.

MEDICAL ORDERLY A soldier with some medical training.

MESS TIN A soldier's cooking pot.

MINE A large underground chamber packed with explosives, placed under enemy lines by tunnellers, or sappers.

MOBILIZATION Preparation of troops for active service.

MORALE Strength of purpose, confidence, or faith.

MORSE CODE A code that represents letters of the alphabet by a sequence of dots and dashes, or long and short signals of light or sound. Named after inventor Samuel Morse (1791–1872).

MUNITIONS Stores of weapons and other military equipment.

NEUTRALITY The refusal to take sides.

NO-MAN'S-LAND An area between two opposing forces that has not been captured by either side.

NON-COMBATANT Someone serving but not fighting with the army, such as a chaplain or an army doctor.

PERISCOPE A device fitted with mirrors to allow the user to see things not in his or her direct line of sight.

PROPAGANDA Information intended to convince people of a specific viewpoint – in posters and broadcasts, for example.

RECONNAISSANCE Taking a preliminary look at an area before sending in troops, usually in order to locate the enemy.

RECONNOITRE To survey an area in preparation for a military advance.

RECRUIT Someone who is enlisted into the army.

REGULAR FORCES Soldiers who already belong to the army, rather than conscripts.

British 7.7-mm (0.303-in) Maxim Mark 3 medium machine gun, c. 1902

German stereoscopic periscope

RESERVE FORCES People who are not part of the regular army but have been trained and are ready to be the first extra troops mobilized in an emergency.

RESPIRATOR A device worn over the face to prevent the wearer from breathing in poisonous gas.

RIFLE A long-barrelled gun, fired from shoulder level.

SEAPLANE An aircraft fitted with floats or skis to land on or take off from water.

SHELL An explosive device that is fired, for example from a cannon.

SHELLSHOCK Mental strain or illness suffered by a soldier who has fought in a war.

SHRAPNEL A type of anti-personnel projectile that contained small shot or spherical bullets, usually of lead, with an explosive charge to scatter the shot.

TELEGRAPH A communications device that transmits messages by means of electrical signals along a wire.

TERRORIST Someone who commits violent acts for political aims.

TORPEDO A self-propelled underwater missile fired from a boat or submarine.

TRENCH A ditch dug by soldiers for protection against enemy fire.

TRUCE An agreement to stop fighting.

U-BOAT A German submarine.

ULTIMATUM A final demand which, if it is not met, results in serious consequences and a total breakdown of communication.

WAR BOND A certificate issued by a government in return for the investment of a sum of money. The money raised helps pay for the war, and is repaid later with interest.

WAR OF ATTRITION Continuous attacks to wear down the enemy.

WIRELESS A communications device that sends messages as radio signals.

Index

Acknowledgements

Dorling Kindersley would like to thank:
Elizabeth Bowers, Christopher Dowling, Mark
Pindelski, & the photography archive team at
the Imperial War Museum for their invaluable
help; Right Section, Kings Own Royal Horse
Artillery for firing the gun shown on page 10;
Lynn Bresler for the index; the author for
assisting with revisions; Claire Bowers, David
Ball, Neville Graham, Rose Horridge, Joanne
Little, and Susan Nicholson for the wallchart;
BCP, Marianne Petrou, and Owen Peyton Jones
for checking the digitized files.

For this relaunch edition, the publishers would
also like to thank: Camilla Hallinan for text
editing and Carron Brown for proofreading.

The publishers would also like to thank the
following for their kind permission to reproduce
their photographs:
a=above, b=below, c=centre, l=left, r=right, t=top

AKG London: 61, 7crb, 36br, 37bl, 38cl, 38bl, 41 tr,
42c, 42bl, 43br, 38cl, 38bl, 41tr, 42c, 42bl, 43br, 52cl,
58–59tl, 60c. Bovington Tank Museum: 68ca.
Bridgeman Art Library, London/New York: ©
Royal Hospital Chelsea, London, UK 67tr. Corbis:
2tr, 6tr, 7tr, 20tr, 22tr, 31tr; Bettmann 8tr, 26–27,
44–45c, 49bl, 55tr, 35bc, 49tl, 54bl, 55t, 55bc, 58–59,
61cr, 69br; Randy Faris 64–65; Christel
Gerstenberg 64tr; Dallas and John Heaton 68bl;
Dave G. Houser 41cr; © Hulton-Deutsch
Collection 66br; Michael St Maur Sheil 70–71
bckgrd; Swim Ink 71tl. DK Picture Library: Andrew
L. Chernack, Springfield, Pennsylvania: 3tr, 55tr;
Imperial War Museum 2cr, 13cl, 20bl, 20br, 27bc,
28cl, 41c, 50bc, 51c, 70bc, 71tr, 71bl, 71br; National
Army Museum: 44bl; RAF Museum, Hendon:
34cla, 34cl; Spink and Son Ltd: 3tl, 4tr, 43bc.
Robert Harding Picture Library: 63c.
Heeresgeschichtliches Museum, Wien: 8bl. Hulton
Getty: 14tl, 17tl, 19br, 21br, 33tr, 32–33b, 35clb,
36cra, 41c, 43t, 47cra, 50clb, 51cl, 58tl, 60tl, 60b,

61tr, 61b; Topical Press Agency 50cl. Imperial
War Museum: 2tl, 8tl (HU68062), 9bl (Q81763),
lltr (Q70075), 10–llt (Q70232), 12clb (32002),
14bc (Q42033), 15tr (Cat. No. 0544), 15cr (Q823),
16c (Q57228), 16b (Q193), 17br (E(AUS)957),
18tr (CO2533), 18cl (Q2953), 18cr (IWM90/62/6),
18br (IWM90/62/4), The Menin Road by Paul
Nash 19tr (Cat. No. 2242), 19cla, 19cr, 19clb
(Q872), 21tc (IWM90/62/5), 21tr (IWM90/62/3),
22bca, 22bl (CO1414), 23t (Q1462), 23br (Q8477),
24tl (Q54985), 24c, 26bl (Q104), 27tl (E921),
26–27b (Q3214), 28cr, 29tr (Q1561), 29br (Q739),
28–29b (Q53), 30tr (Q1778), 30cl (Q2628), 31br
(Q4502), 321, 32c (Q8537), 33tl (Q30678), 33tr
(1646), 33cr (Q19134), 35cb (Q42284), 35bl
(Q69593), 34–35c, 36clb, 37 (Q27488), 38tl, 38tr
(PST0515), 39cr (Q20883), 39br (Q63698), 40cl
(Q13618), 40br (Q13281), 41tl (Q13603), 41b
(Q13637), 45br (Q55085), Gassed by John Singer
Sargent 44–45b (1460), 48cr (Q60212), 48bl, 51tr
(Q26945), 52bl (Q9364), 53cr (Q6434), 53br (Q9364),
54tl (2747), Sappers at Work by David Bomberg
56cl (2708), 57tr (E(AUS)1396), 57cr (Q5935),
56–57c (Q754), 56–57b (Q2708), 58b (Q10810),
59tr (Q9534), 59b (Q9586), The Signing of Peace
in the Hall of Mirrors, Versailles by Sir William

Orpen 61tl (2856), 62tl (Q2756), 62c Q1540), 64cla
(Q30788), 64crb (Q50671), 64bc (Q4834), 65clb
(Q10956), 65br (Q609), 66cr (Q949), 66cla (Q54534),
66bl (Q66377), 67tl (Q7302), 67clb (Q9631), 67br
(Q1582), 69bl (IWM 90-62-3), 70tl (Q27814), 70cr
(Q26946); David King Collection: 46bl, 47tl, 58cla.
Kobal Collection: Columbia 69tl. National Gallery
Of Canada, Ottawa: Transfer from the Canadian
War Memorials, Dazzle ships in dry dock at
Liverpool, 1921 by Edward Wadsworth 39tl. Peter
Newark's Military Pictures: 13ac, 42tr. Pa Photos:
European Press Agency 65t. Popperfoto: Reuters
68br. Roger-Viollet: 9tr, 9cr, llbr, 13cr, 19tl; Boyer
17bl. Telegraph Colour Library: J.P. Fruchet 62c.
Topham Picturepoint: 42tl, 46tl, 47br, 46–47b, 62b;
ASAP 43cl. Ullstein Bild: 8–9c, 46tr.

Wallchart credits:
Corbis: Bettmann br, tr

All other images © Dorling Kindersley.
For further information see:
www.dkimages.com